The Bonham Brothers' Boys Band

The Bonham Brothers' Boys Band

William Ward Martin

Spaceland Publications Co.

San Diego, California

The Bonham Brothers' Boys Band

An Excerpt From:

Adventures in an Age of Innocence

Spaceland Publications Co.
San Diego, California
October, 2009

HARLEY L. BONHAM

Harley L Bonham

B. W. BONHAM

B. W. Bonham

Bonham Brothers' Band Pledge

   I, *the Undersigned,* member of Bonham Brothers' Band, do hereby pledge myself to abstain from the use of profane language, and all habits that do not make the best of manhood. To be honest in all my dealings and in all my thoughts, always telling the truth without fear.

  I pledge myself to keep my body physically, morally and spiritually clean, to forgive those that hurt me, to help and protect the weak, the young and the old; to love my parents, my home, my neighbors and my country and be loyal to all these.

  I further pledge myself to work for better grades in my school, to support my Sunday School by regular attendance, to be polite and courteous at all times and strive for harmony, not only in my playing, but also in my organization by good behavior and deportment.

  All this I sincerely pledge, realizing that I must build my character by training myself in good habits, thus becoming a better citizen.

B. W. Bonham

JULES F. JACQUES, *Director*
BONHAM BROTHERS' BAND

Bonham Brothers' Boys Band

Mr. Myron Collins ruled with a rod of iron, and I was terrified of him. There he sat in his chair, inches away from me, pot bellied, bespectacled, a man possessed. Nothing mattered to him outside the one great passion of his life: teaching boys the snare drum. To his few charges (he interviewed his students before taking them on) he was almost like God. I mean, if you failed to practice he'd know it; there'd be a different look in his eye when he greeted you at his door. That was when my face started burning and I knew I was in for sixty minutes of hell.

One day Mr. Collins put his hand on my shoulder and said, "Bill, I've recommended you to Mr. Jules Jacques of the Bonham Brothers' Boys Band. He is the greatest living band conductor in the country. I expect you to do well."

My knees shook the night my parents took me to meet the great conductor. There were trophies everywhere in his house and on the walls there were plaques and photographs of dignitaries and past bands. After shaking hands with my parents he asked me back to his private den where he seated me at a small writing desk and took a chair opposite. His face was tanned and he had wavy brown hair and there were little brown specks in his hazel eyes. He held up a gold watch chain. "Do you know how strong this chain is, son?"

"No sir."

"As strong as its weakest link."

He held the chain steady and watched me. "A band, son, is no different from this chain. If a boy misses a note or marches out of step the order that holds the band together will be broken. Do you understand?"

"Yes, sir."

"Mr. Collins says you're one of his best students. How would you like to play the bass drum? It's the heartbeat of our band."

"Yes, sir. Thank you, sir."

He must have liked what he saw in me because the next day a newspaper man took a picture of us together to publicize the organizing of our new 150-piece Bonham Brothers' Boys Band. It thrilled me very much to be photographed with Mr. Jacques and when the photograph appeared in the *Shopping News and News-Press* on February 20, 1946 the public got to look at a wide-eyed boy strapped to an enormous bass drum with Mr. Jacques standing behind him and holding his hands in "the approved method of beating the drums."

Our first meeting as a band took place on the night of March 22, 1946 in the chapel of the Bonham Brothers' Mortuary at Fourth and Elm in downtown San Diego. It was sort of creepy having undertakers for sponsors and when Mr. Bonham told us about all the bands that had gone before us and how being in the new band would make us better citizens by moral, physical and spiritual training, I couldn't help thinking about how there must be dead bodies just beyond the lily-painted wall behind him, all lying face-up in their coffins and waiting for their funerals.

Mr. Bonham had a big bald head and when he spoke he shook all over like there was something wrong with him. It made me think of all the dead bodies he'd worked on and how this was probably the cause of his shaking, and I started to feel sorry for him and hoped that people wouldn't think of our band as a bunch of little marchers for the dead. Mr. Bonham said our band was the first to be organized since before the war and was the seventh to be organized in San Diego since the first one had been formed in 1926. Its conductor, he said, was Mr. Jacques. Mr. Jacques had taken over the band in 1929 and since then over a thousand boys had experienced the advantage of fine band training and the thrill of public appearances in gala events.

Pretty soon I wasn't thinking about dead people anymore but about all the bands that Mr. Bonham had mentioned. They had won many big contests in San Diego, and in plenty of other big cities too, like the Lion's International contest in Oakland, and the All-Western Band review in Long Beach, in which they had won the sweepstakes in a field of sixty bands. One band had distinguished itself by marching in the rain during one of the Tournament of Roses Parades. Another had even played before one of the presidents of the United States. Many of the band members had gone on to make big names for themselves. One, whose name was Dominick Buono, played four years with the Harry James band and was now the first trumpet in the Bob Crosby band. Another, Frank Comstock, who had played trombone, was an arranger for the big swing bands.

I stole a glance at all the kids and parents, then at my mother and father who were dressed up and looking proud. Everyone was looking straight at Mr. Bonham. There were band members, he went on, who had been decorated for valor and bravery during the war. Others owned music stores, and still others taught at West Point or at Harvard, or else were doctors or lawyers. Then topping everything off Mr. Bonham told us about Mr. Jacques. He was already famous, he said, and could play the trumpet and would be our leader for the next four years. We were very lucky to be under his charge and we were to obey him to the letter.

Then Mr. Bonham backed away and Mr. Jacques came forward. He was very handsome and confident-looking and when he began to speak my mother gave me a little nudge. I could tell she liked him and it made me proud that I already knew him and had been alone with him in his private study and that he had given his little talk to me about the gold chain. We would start out by following the usual plan, he said, learning how to play our instruments in our respective sections. During the summer months we'd rehearse three mornings a week as a full band. Our rehearsals would be shifted to the afternoon once school started.

Anybody could see that Mr. Jacques was a real man. When he spoke, his voice sounded full of authority and his eyes didn't miss anything as he looked around the room, and when they came to mine it seemed like it was just me and him. You could've heard a pin drop. Then he began to talk about the band's motto and pledge which had been handed out to us. We were expected to practice at least one half hour each day, he said, except on Sundays. We were to take proper care of our instruments. We were to arrive at rehearsals looking clean and neat. We were to be polite and courteous at all times. We must not be late or absent from rehearsals or engagements more than three times, without a reasonable excuse from our parents. And we weren't to play for any other organization unless we had his permission. Any boy who did not obey the rules would be dismissed from the band, he said.

Then he told us we were to learn the Bonham Brothers' pledge and then sign it in ink which made me think of sacred oaths and blood bonds between kings and knights and other chivalrous things I'd read about in my Junior Classics funny books. Mr. Jacques paused for a moment as though he knew he had said enough. Then he smiled and told us that a great tradition preceded us. In nine months we'd be ready to make our public debut. Then he congratulated us all and gave a little bow and I could feel chills going up and down my spine, and that was that. I went home feeling proud and important.

The Bonham Brothers' rehearsal hall was a wooden-floored, wooden-walled basement in Mr. Jacques's home on Sixth Avenue in Hillcrest. A worn platform around the north and east walls where the sousaphone, percussion and trombone sections were assigned. Below the platform on the west side of the room sat the clarinet and accordion sections. In the middle of the room sat all the flute, saxophone and baritone players. The trumpet section was put on Mr. Jacques's immediate right, directly under his watchful eye.

That summer we practiced for the first time in the famous bandroom. It seemed a thousand ghosts were with us and you could see where the feet of earlier band members had been because the wood was worn where they had sat. There was a cozy smell in the air, too, as though the air in the room had been preserved to hold in all the memories and make our music better. We showed up on time too, because that's what it said in our band motto, and at home we practiced at least one half-hour each day except on Sundays. We also took proper care of our instruments and never arrived for rehearsals without being clean and neat, as well as polite and courteous at all times.

Slowly but surely Jacques made us into a band: our trombones came together, the trumpet players started hitting their high notes, the tubas umpaughed out the beats, and the woodwinds keyed off the brass while we of the Collins tradition flammed and rolled and drove everyone on. It wasn't too long before the walls of the bandroom were resounding to the strains of Bennett's "Military Escort" and John Philip Sousa's "Washington Post."

That summer Jacques took us to the Roosevelt Junior High School parade grounds to teach us how to march as a band. At first we felt self-conscious about being in the public eye. I mean, there were cars zooming by on Park Boulevard to the east, and to the west there were people visiting the camel and llama exhibits of the world famous San Diego Zoo. But we soon got used to things and how it was actually fun marching next to the zoo with all its animals and the peacocks crying and all the visitors looking at us through the tall wire fences, especially when we could see the beautiful buildings of Balboa Park rising up behind them.

The park was very famous. It had its California Tower with a giant bell that tolled the time. There was a natural history museum too, and a museum of man, and hundreds of tall eucalyptus trees everywhere. Plus there was a huge open-air bowl for concerts, and an organ pavilion where Winston Churchill once spoke, and a great statue of El Cid sitting on a horse, and a famous botanical garden and a giant lily pond and a beautiful fountain, plus a merry-go-round and all kinds of other important things which were left over from the world famous expositions in 1916 and 1935. It made us all very proud to be learning how to march as a band with all these things nearby and pretty soon we began to feel like we were part of the city. Soon we'd be a real marching band and by Christmas we'd be ready to make our concert debut, just as Mr. Jacques had said.

It was great having Mr. Jacques teaching us how to march. I had never seen a man walk so proud as he could. His chest stuck out like he owned the world and when he was marching he brought his arms forward and then snapped them across his body. His head never moved either. Watching him made us all want to strut the same way except we couldn't because of our instruments and because it was tricky learning how to play and walk at the same time.

Up and down the parade grounds he drilled us, now at our rear, now on our flanks, now marching backwards up in front, his eagle eyes missing nothing. When he barked out commands our hearts beat faster than normal and our fingers tingled. Sometimes he'd rush into our midst, spanking instruments up, pulling stragglers back into alignment with their fellows, or leaning his head over to hear if a boy's instrument was in tune. At other times he'd blow us to a halt with his whistle. There in the saxophone section, and over there in the last row of the clarinet section—two boys out of step! We all stood and watched as he called the offenders out of formation and marched them back and forth until they no longer had their feet tangled. Then with a blast of his whistle we were off again, marching to the rolling and flamming of our drum section. West Point marchers he wanted. A band was more than just music. The eye must be satisfied as well as the ear.

No breech with Jacques was treated lightly. One day he stepped off his podium and leaned into the second row of the trumpet section and snatched a trumpet out of a boy's hand. "I will not allow bad habits in my band," he exclaimed. "A drooping trumpet is the mark of a lazy musician. You will hold your instrument parallel to the floor or I will send you home with a note to your parents that you are too tired to play."

Like Mr. Collins, Jacques had no truck with slackards or mediocrities. One drummer who made a habit of missing practices he simply kicked out of the band. Three times we saw him storm through whole sections, knocking over music stands, to upbraid a boy for not paying attention. And woe betide the poor unfortunate if he didn't acknowledge his lapse and apologize to the rest of us. On other occasions he simply waved his trumpet in the air, then blew out a passage to make us rise above ourselves.

Jacques had an ear for the slightest mistake. If any of us played out of tune or off the beat we'd hear the tapping of the baton. There, in the third row of the clarinet section, fourth boy in from the right. What was the problem? Failure to practice? Well then, he would stand up and get it right. And god help the boy if he couldn't.

Occasionally Mr. Jacques would praise, and when he did, the happy recipient was the envy of the whole band. Once, when our first trumpeter got through a difficult riff, he stopped the band and, motioning for the boy to stand, asked him to play the passage again. When he obliged without a hitch, Jacques turned to us and said, very slowly and very quietly, "That's how to do it." We were his slaves for life.

By December 1946, we were ready for our debut. Our parents dipped into their savings, drove us downtown to be fitted for our band uniforms, and after six long months of rehearsals the great moment was upon us.

On the fated night we dressed up in our new uniforms, got help from our fathers with our neckties, and after a quick look in the mirror were taken by our parents to the massive First Methodist Church at Ninth and C Streets in downtown San Diego. There was no doubt that it was the biggest night of our lives. Nearly a thousand people were to be in the audience to hear us perform a real live official concert. At the back stage entrance of the church clusters of parents and friends were standing by to wish us encouragement. Inside we set up our music stands behind the church's tall burgundy-colored stage curtains and found our places to sit. I felt a little trembly. Everyone else was too.

Right off we could hear the growing hum of conversation on the other side of the stage curtains. Nobody felt like saying much. Somewhere in the balcony a man coughed. Bright stage lights blazed down on us. After a little bit a boy in the trombone section lifted his instrument up and tuned it with a few soft notes. Then another boy followed in the clarinet section, then other boys in other sections cautiously tested their instruments as though they might offend the growing audience on the other side of the stage curtains. After a while someone made a hushing sound up front and the audience quieted, and we all came to attention in our chairs. Then the curtain suddenly began drawing apart with a clicking rushing sound and we were facing a black void and a thousand unseen eyes.

A hundred forty hearts are pounding as applause breaks the silence in a crescendoing welcome. Then everything suddenly goes blank like being in a dream and there's nowhere to hide, no going back. Then we see him. It's Mr. Jacques entering the stage from the wing on our right. He's wearing a white conductor's suit and looking very tanned and handsome. We watch as he strides to the lectern, turns and faces the audience, makes a bow, then about-faces and steps up onto the conductor's platform. All eyes are on him as he reaches for his white baton, turns his musical score to the first page, looks up, taps his baton on the edge of the podium, slowly lifts it, holds us for a second, then flashing a big smile brings it down with a flourish and we're off and running in our first number, all our fears suddenly vanished, music sheets back in focus, and the audience and the night and the whole wide world ours for the taking.

Had Jacques planned this priceless moment? At this distance I shall never know. But in that unforgettable moment, in the flash of his smile, he had rescued us from fear and made us into something we'd never been before.

After our triumphant debut, Jacques began to prepare us for the granddaddy of all concerts, the annual open-air Easter Sunday concert in Balboa Park's Ford Bowl. Billed as the seventeenth annual Easter Sunday concert given by the Bonham

Brothers' Boys Band, it was expected to draw over 3,500 people. Jacques had three months to get us ready.

Three times a week we descended the wooden stairs to the bandroom where Jacques took us beyond where we had been in our last practice; advancing us measure by measure, instrument by instrument, boy by boy, section by section. Rough edges disappeared, notes were hit truer, sections fused into more sonorous harmonies with each other. Then one afternoon in the last week of March Jacques gave us a congratulatory nod and we knew we were ready. We had mastered an impressive list of marches and overtures. What's more, we had succeeded in blessing them with the style and spirit of our great teacher.

On Sunday April 6, 1947 we got dressed in our formal concert blue and white uniforms and prepared our minds to show the world who we now were. Our program featured "Onward Christian Soldiers" and "Adeste Fidelis," the overtures "Mt. Everest" and "Ambition," and the great American march favorites "Military Escort," "Activity," and "Washington Post." To these were added an invocation, solos from our drum and saxophone sections, a harp solo by a Miss Ruth Negri, and vocals of sacred music by Mr. Don A. Smith with accompaniment from Miss Diana Quint. After that came the recital of the Bonham Brothers' Band Pledge, the only feature on the program that struck terror in me. The program read:

Bonham Brothers' Band Pledge:
Recited by WILLIAM MARTIN

It had taken twelve weeks to memorize and master the band pledge. Twenty-eight lines. One hundred sixty-eight words.

Recited at every practice session to all the band members and Mr. Jacques from Christmas down to the last rehearsal before Easter Sunday; recited to my mother and father at the dinner table each night; recited on the way to and from school; recited to my friend Donnie Foster up the street; recited to Dickie Archibald and his little brother Jimmy, and even recited to my brother Terry below my bunk bed every night. Gradually I had fought off the demons of fear, but you could never tell when they'd come back to haunt you between recitings. To this day I cringe at the memory of saying those lines in front of all those thousands of people under that bright Easter Sunday sunshine in the Ford Bowl:

Bonham Brothers' Band Pledge

I, the Undersigned, member of Bonham Brothers' Band, do hereby pledge myself to abstain from the use of profane language, and all habits that do not make the best of manhood. To be honest in all my dealings and in all my thoughts, always telling the truth without fear.

I pledge myself to keep my body physically, morally and spiritually clean, to forgive those that hurt me, to help and protect the weak, the young and the old; to love my parents, my home, my neighbors and my country and be loyal to all these.

I further pledge myself to work for better grades in my school, to support my Sunday School by regular attendance, to be polite and courteous at all times and strive for harmony, not only in my playing, but also in my organization by good behavior and deportment.

All this I sincerely pledge, realizing that I must build my character by training myself in good habits, thus becoming a better citizen.

It happened like this. The band was in the shadow of the enormous stage backing. Bright sunlight flooded the bowl and stage out front. The audience, dressed in their Sunday best, had overflowed the bowl.

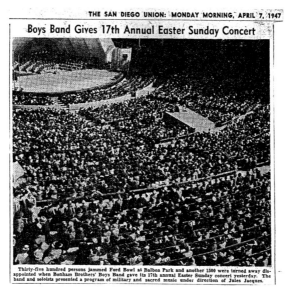

THE SAN DIEGO UNION: MONDAY MORNING, APRIL 7, 1947

Boys Band Gives 17th Annual Easter Sunday Concert

Thirty-five hundred persons jammed Ford Bowl at Balboa Park and another 1500 were turned away disappointed when Bonham Brothers' Boys Band gave its 17th annual Easter Sunday concert yesterday. The band and soloists presented a program of military and sacred music under direction of Jules Jacques.

My eyes were glazed as I rehearsed the pledge's opening lines. We played a march, then an overture, then another march, then another overture. I half heard the accordion and xylophone solos that followed. Then a woman came out and played a harp followed by a man and a woman who sang some holy songs. The band played another march. I stared numbly out into the sea of people during the program's "Operatic Mingle." I felt out of my body like in a dream or something. To this day I feel this sensation when recalling that ghastly moment. For I was next.

Our master of ceremony rises from his chair in the saxophone section and marches snappily out to the mike. His lines are flawlessly memorized. He is born for his role. "And now, ladies and gentlemen, to recite our band pledge—"

Benumbed, the boy makes his way forward through the band to the huge sun-washed proscenium. From there he strikes out for the mike that seems half a block away. An ocean of faces awaits him. He reaches the mike, comes to attention, and remembers to keep his arms straight down at his sides and his head facing somewhere in the middle of the audience. He begins: "I, the undersigned, member of the Bonham Brothers' Greater San Diego Band, do hereby pledge myself to abstain from the use of profane language and all habits that do not make the best of manhood." A man is wearing a tan coat up in the middle section. Is it Randolph Scott the movie actor? Next to him a lady is wearing a giant Easter bonnet. Could she be his wife? "To be honest in all my dealings and in all my thoughts, always telling the truth without fear." To the man's left three teenage girls are sitting side-by-side. The one in the middle is cuter than the other two. Are they already in Junior High? "To love my parents, my home, my neighbors and my country." Over to the right some people are perched up in a tree watching. Some more people are seated on the top of a wall. "I further pledge myself to work for better grades in my school, to support my Sunday School by regular attendance."

He blinks in the bright sunlight and sees his aunt Agnes. What is she doing here? Is Uncle Al with her? The pledge— the pledge! He's gotten through the first two paragraphs and now the third. Or has he? He recites the third just in case, then goes on to the fourth. Then it's all over and everyone is applauding and he's marching back to take his place in the band.

Did he say the third paragraph twice? He threads his way past the saxophone and trombone sections to his seat behind the bass drum and sinks into despair. There's no doubt about it. He could see the answer in one of the baritone player's eyes. He said the stupid thing twice! How can he face his fellow band members? How can he face Mr. Jacques? How can he face his parents? Or his aunt and uncle, or the audience or anyone?

A saxophone solo follows, then a march, then the band is playing "The Star Spangled Banner," the concert's finale. He's in a hopeless daze now. When the famous anthem reaches its climax he swings his mallet and misses the cymbal altogether, leaving a ghostly silence that fills the vast Ford Bowl. On Easter Sunday! Under the gaze of God and all his angels in heaven! In front of all the people in the audience! In front of the newspaper reporters! In front of all the dignitaries! In front of the whole world and everyone!

He never really believed the third paragraph. So why did he say it twice? There was always something wrong with it, that's why, said the old familiar voice—the voice that always said at the critical moment in church, "God is shit, God is shit, God is shit." Maybe it made him say it twice because he was just a little eleven year old hypocrite telling a big lie to all those thousands of people on Easter Sunday. All his life he would remember that lie he told twice; the lie that sabotaged what everybody else thought was noble and right and that in his own heart he knew was wrong.

> I further pledge myself to work for better grades in my school, to support my Sunday School by regular attendance, to be polite and courteous at all times and strive for harmony, not only in my playing, but also in my organization by good behavior and deportment.

Jacques never said anything. Nor did anyone in the band. It was my father who said it. I was sitting on the back seat of the family car on the way home and looking out at all the eucalyptus trees in the park going by when he remarked without looking back, "Son, I noticed you repeated one of the paragraphs." His words struck me like a meat cleaver. I wanted to die. I was ashamed of my uniform. I hated the band. I hated the concert. I hated Easter Sunday. I hated the car. I hated the late afternoon sunlight streaming through the window. Not even the park's merry-go-round passing by outside seemed fun anymore. It was then my mother turned around in the front seat. She looked me straight in the eye.

"Honey, nobody's going to remember that paragraph. Why, you just overmastered that thing. Now let me tell you something. Your sentences were pronounced just beautifully. And your voice was strong and clear. And let me tell you something else. Those people in that audience will never again see an eleven-year-old boy with a stage presence like you had today. You were just magnificent."

She held me with her eyes after she finished and I loved her for getting the last word over my father. But it didn't make the hurt go away, even if I believed her, and knew she was right.

After my disaster there was nowhere to go but up. The band pledge was behind me and so was my missing of the stupid cymbal and I knew I would never be asked to publicly recite anything ever again in my whole life. With every practice session after that my confidence grew, and not only that, my authority with the bass drum began to permeate the whole band.

One day Jacques took me aside and said that I would be playing bass drum in the "little band" that he was forming for special functions where the big band would be out of place. It was quite an honor and by the end of the first week in May I was providing the heartbeat of the band as never before.

On May 11 we played an afternoon concert under the famous eucalyptus trees of Balboa Park. It was the first time we all got to wear our gray marching trousers with black shoes and stockings and it made us proud that we were making the in-between step to being in our first parade. After the concert my father took a picture of me standing next to the base drum,

then another one with my brother and little sister, and then one of my mother who was wearing a wide-brimmed hat and looked very proud and beautiful. The crowds took pictures of us too, and no one wanted to leave and all the people looked just wonderful in their Sunday best.

After that we were booked solid. On Saturday, May 17 we were honored with the privilege of playing martial music at the Broadway Pier for the third commissioning of the famous light cruiser *Astoria*. It had been a World War II warship and had never lost a man from enemy action despite its great battles against the Japs at Formosa, Luzon, and the South China Coast, and later with the Fifth Fleet at Iwo Jima and Okinawa.

It made me feel important standing under its tall, patriotic-looking gray bow and pounding out "Anchor's Away" on the Bonham Band's beautiful blue-and-white bass drum. Every other boy in the band felt the same way as we stood at attention and played our instruments, knowing that we were public figures now, even patriots, making real history that would be written up in the newspapers instead of just being little kids fighting Japs down in the canyons and on vacant lots.

A week after we played "Anchors Away" for the *Astoria* we gladdened the hearts of a huge afternoon crowd of parents and boys at the Boy Scout Camporee in Balboa Park. Everybody just loved us. It made me feel superior too. I mean, I was in the band instead of just being a graduated cub scout wasting the whole day pitching tents and doing other dumb little projects. Then at the end of May we got to march in our first parade, looking like West Point cadets and hearing waves of applause from throngs of spectators in the City of San Diego's big Memorial Day Parade. The next night, May 31, the little band performed its first concert for the Hi Twelve at the Silvergate Masonic Temple and Lodge in North Park. Everyone in the audience knew we were the best players in the band, and we didn't disappoint them either. What's more, midway through our concert Mr. Harley Bonham came up on the stage out of the audience and gave an impromptu talk. He was very happy with our band, he said. He told the audience that we were learning to be better citizens among boys, and that our progress as musicians was inspiring. He was very proud to see us promoting civic interest, too, and how this boosted San Diego. Then, suddenly, he turned his back to the audience and pointed up into the band to me and asked that I come forward to the microphone.

Me? My heart pounded as I stepped down from the drummer's platform and made my way through the band toward the open stage. Why me? There were other boys who were more dedicated to their music. Then I was out on the stage under all the lights and Mr. Bonham had his hand on my shoulder and was pulling me closer to him. I tried to keep from squinting. Mr. Bonham was saying something about my being a model band member or something. Then I felt sad that my parents weren't able to come to the concert that night. Then my mind drifted off and I was listening to my grandmother on that long ago Easter Eve of 1940. "Mark my words, Babesie, he'll be a great man someday."

Our next engagement was on opening day, June 27, at the San Diego County Fair in Del Mar. Summer vacation had just begun and we all felt freer and happier. We took to Stage B at 2:30 that afternoon and played to a packed audience, and then on the same stage at 7:00 that same evening. We could see people and families coming and going beyond the bleachers and the Ferris wheel turning in the distance and all the time the summer breeze was blowing and you could smell the sea in it. That night Lt. Governor Goodwin J. Knight pulled a switch that lit the fairgrounds up all pretty and bright. There were all kinds of things to see and do, too. There were pet shows, and "Serrano" the World's Best Educated Horse, and rodeos, and "Li'l Doug" the Wonder Bear, and colorful Shrine circuses, plus the famous "Queen for a Day" radio show had come to the Fair, along with "Previews of Progress" by General Motors. To top things off we were given special admission permits that gave us the run of all exhibits and discounts on the carnival acts and rides from morning to midnight.

After the Del Mar Fair it seemed like we played at all the public events in San Diego, because the very next day, June 28, we were marching in our first parade down Broadway to the Santa Fe Train Depot where we ended up playing a standing concert before a waiting crowd. Then it was the Fourth of July holiday weekend and we were playing a concert for the first time in beautiful Balboa Stadium at the San Diego Fireman's Annual Fireworks Show. The firemen put on a huge circus after we played and I got to sit up in the stadium with my family in my band uniform. The trapeze girls were the best. Their bodies were just perfect and it made me sad watching them and I wanted to run away with them and have them take care of me and be in love with me and not be jealous with each other or anything. After the circus came the fireworks, and I wondered where the trapeze girls were and if they were watching all the starry bursts of color in the night. When I went to bed later I could still see their beautiful arms and legs and how brave they were and I wondered if they felt sad like me.

All the rest of July Mr. Jacques taught us new marches in the band hall, and drove us to new heights of harmony and pride. When August rolled around he again presented us to the public: the five-mile-long "Days of '49" parade in Chula Vista led by Lt. Governor Knight and Mayor L. C. Koester (August 16); a little band concert for the Elks Club in Balboa

Park's Pepper Grove (August 24); and a National City parade honoring the Olympic Games (August 30).

It was hard to tell which was better, the parades or the concerts. In the parades you could see a lot of things happening and people waving at you and horses and motorcycle cops and clowns. It was fun dodging all the horse droppings without getting out of formation or the crowds noticing. Some of the piles smoked as you went by and I don't know why it was but I thought they smelled fresh and wholesome. The concerts were different. You didn't have things to look at much but that was made up for by the fact that you didn't have to lug around a heavy instrument or sweat or get sore feet like when you marched in parades. Besides, Mr. Jacques said that we were beginning to have the makings of his best concert band ever. So, when you got down to it the concerts were better.

After our National City parade, Mr. Jacques withdrew us from the public again for the whole month of September to prepare us for our big fall schedule. All month long we practiced. We learned two new marches, a medley and two overtures, and everyone began talking about how we were becoming Mr. Jacques's best band ever.

Earlier that summer my father moved us into a tract house on 42nd Street on the southeast side of San Diego. It was only temporary, he said, until he could find us a house that was closer to his work. He was sorry about the location but it was necessary on account of the housing shortage that had been caused by the war.

There were colored people in our new neighborhood and a lot of Mexicans and only a few white people. It made me pretty scared to live there because the Negro kids were mean and tough and liked to pick fights whenever they had the chance. I was lucky that I didn't have to transfer to Chollas Elementary school. I'd already been kicked out of one school and I guess the authorities figured once was enough and that I was big enough now to take the bus into town and then up Fifth Avenue to Florence Elementary for the final weeks of school. My little brother Terry wasn't so lucky though. Every day he got threatened and bullied and he lived in terror.

Living in southeast San Diego was probably a good experience though. I mean, it made me stand up more than ever to bullies, no matter who they were. One day a tall skinny Negro boy fingered me out of a line of kids waiting to see a Frankenstein movie at the Chollas recreation center and heaved an orange at me. I dodged it and something went crazy inside me and I ran and picked up the orange where it had fallen at the base of the recreation building and hurled it back with everything I had, scoring a direct hit smack in the middle of the boy's chest. The orange splattered everywhere and before we could get into a fight a white man stepped outside the recreation building and blew a whistle for us to get back in line. Later, inside the theater the nigger found me and slipped into the seat next to me. His name was Leroy, he said. What was mine? I told him and he shook my hand and said we should be friends because I wasn't afraid of him.

I took him home afterwards and introduced him to my mother. He told her he was going to be my brother's bodyguard. My mother made us peanut butter sandwiches. I could tell she liked him because he was funny and because his mind was sharp and he noticed things. After he left she said we were probably the first white family he had ever been true friends with. But my friendship with Leroy didn't last. We moved away to Point Loma where my father was working at the High Seas Tuna Packing Company and I never saw him again.

Our new house in Point Loma was on a steep hill overlooking San Diego Bay. A few blocks away was a place called Jenning's Beach where I started teaching myself the Johnny Weismuller crawl stroke like I'd seen in the Tarzan movies. It was neat being free to ride my bike down to the bay and see and smell all the boats and to go fishing off the piers and to see the old Portuguese men standing around talking, and to be close to where my father worked at the cannery.

The people in our neighborhood spoke Portuguese. They were part of the great tuna fishing business and when they talked they used their hands a lot and were loud and didn't seem at all like Americans. The boys were good at sports and they could run fast and were good swimmers and they didn't have any freckles. When they went to the beach they got really good tans and sometimes I wished I were Portuguese so I wouldn't have any freckles.

The Portuguese boys were clannish and tough and it was hard to make friends with them. Some of them talked dirty and knew stuff about girls I'd never dreamed of. But I knew I could make them respect me once I tried out for their American Legion baseball team over on Cabrillo playground, which was only three blocks away. As for the Portuguese girls, they could be prettier than a lot of the American girls I'd seen. But you could tell they were saving themselves for the Portuguese boys when they got older because they never looked at me. But I shrugged it off, although sometimes it made me admit to myself that I was inferior in looks and maybe in some other things too that I didn't know about. Then again, the Portuguese were Catholics and I'd definitely gone way past them in that.

Before I knew it summer was over just like all the other summers and I was enrolled in Dana Junior High School high up on the top of the Point behind our house. I could have ridden my bike to school, but then why do that when there was a footpath to school through the brush-covered hills behind our house where you could look at the bay and the city of San Diego. It was without any doubt the best way to start the school day off because it kept me thinking of nature during first period class and sometimes even my second period class before the stuffy air and boring teachers made me fidgety and helpless and tired feeling like in my elementary school days.

For a few days Dana Junior High seemed sort of neat because I had different classes to go to instead of being cooped up in the same room all day. Plus I had a couple of man teachers. But it wore off pretty quick. School was school. What's more, my male teachers didn't act or look very much like men. When you got right down to it, they might just as well have been schoolmarms. You could tell that by the way they took attendance and went by the rules. But hiking to school up over the hills in the mornings with the sun on my neck and smelling the weeds and seeing the blue sky above and the bay and city and mountains behind me definitely helped me to get through at least part of the day.

As soon as school was out I hit the trail back down over the Point toward home. Way below I could see the sailboats and ships in the bay. There were rattlers in the brush alongside the trail too, and it was fun to be on the lookout for them. Then I was dropping down onto Carleton Street with it's steep hill where we lived and deciding whether I should play tag football over on Cabrillo playground, or zoom down to the bay on my bike to get better at swimming, or cruise over to the cannery where stuff was always going on.

Everything outside of school was better and more important. Sometimes I got neat little chills just thinking about going to sea on a freighter or on a tunaboat or becoming a big league ballplayer or just about anything at all out in the world of business—fireman, ditch digger, cannery worker, it didn't matter. Heck, I was already a public figure in my other life in the Bonham Brothers' Boys Band. How could school compare with that? In less than six months I'd promoted more civic interest and boosting of San Diego than all the teachers in all the schools of San Diego could have done in that same time, as far as I was concerned.

All through September Jacques worked on improving us. Our marching formations squared off truer and down in the bandroom the old wooden walls echoed our growing confidence. When October rolled around we were 135 strong, proven veterans of Jacques's first-year purgings, eager to take on another big run of public appearances.

On the tenth of October we marched under the city lights in our parade grays down Broadway in the Elks Parade. All along the sidewalks people waved and cheered and when we passed the Spreckels Theater building a round of applause went up as an official parade car ahead of us announced over a loud-speaker that the Bonham Brothers' Boys Band would once again be escorting San Diego's float in the Rose Parade. The crowds called out well-wishes to us and I saw a couple of moms blowing kisses.

Eight days later, on October 18, we put on our formal concert whites and drove our growing reputation to new heights by playing a rousing afternoon concert for the Kiwanis Convention in San Diego's famous Russ Auditorium where the San Diego Symphony and the city's great operas were performed. A week later we were marching up Broadway again in the Shrine Charity parade to Balboa Stadium where we took part in the pageantry of the tenth annual Al Bahr Shrine Football Game. It was a chilly October night and a heavy fog had settled over the stadium. No one could see a thing. I think everybody liked it though because when we played the National Anthem fifteen thousand spectators stood up and cheered wildly in the direction of the flagpole at the south end of the stadium where Old Glory was being raised unseen to the top of the flagpole. At halftime we played the San Diego Aztec fight song in the fog and all around us we could see where the grass had been kicked up by the football players in the game that no one saw. But no one really cared whether they saw the game or not, because as the newspapers said the next day, the game was played so that "weak legs may walk."

A couple of nights later we were back in Balboa Stadium. The date was October 27, 1947, and the fog was gone. All the stars were out and forty thousand San Diegans were making a record-breaking reception for Fleet Admiral Chester W. Nimitz who had just returned home from the war. The famous admiral gave a short speech praising defenses and urging alertness, and half way up the north end of the stadium you could see thousands of navy Bluejackets spelling out the admiral's name in huge white capital letters. The next day the

Leader of U. S. Sea Forces Receives Applause of Cheering Thousands

Largest throng in history of Balboa Stadium, estimated by police at nearly 40,000 persons, paid honor to Fleet Adm. Chester W. Nimitz in Navy Day program last night. Looking north, this shows massed bands in foreground. Bluejackets spell "Nimitz" in stands.

newspapers said that there were only two other times when the stadium had been filled with so many people. That was when President Wilson came in 1919 and again when President Roosevelt came in 1935. It was great thinking that we had been honored to stand next to the Navy and Marine bands and to play the "Star Spangled Banner," "Anchor's Away" and "The Halls of Montezuma"! It was enough to give you chills, especially when behind our backs, among the giant Doric col-

umns at the south end of the stadium, a huge American flag
hung all glorious and beautiful with its forty-eight stars on it.
On each side there were banners bearing the names of the
great Pacific battles of Pearl Harbor, Guadalcanal, Midway,
Iwo Jima, Okinawa, and Tokyo.

While narrator traced history of the great Battle for the Pacific that Nimitz directed, bluejackets atop the stadium's spotlighted peristyle unfurled banners marking high points of the long campaign. Nimitz warned listeners peacetime U. S. must control ocean lanes.

After that it was a cinch to play for giant crowds, and all the
more so if it was in a place like the Ford Bowl. On Saturday
morning, November 1, 1947 the San Diego Union declared:
"Several thousand San Diegans of Protestant faith are
expected to attend the first all-Protestant observance of Reformation Day at 3 P.M. tomorrow in Ford Bowl, Balboa Park. . .
. Under the direction of Jules Jacques, Bonham Brothers'
Boys Band will play 'Invercargill' by Lithgow; 'Mount Everest
Overture' by Griffen; 'Onward Christian Soldiers,' 'Adeste
Fidelis' and 'Washington Post March.'" The audience wasn't
disappointed either. I mean, we played great and Mr. Jacques
even gave me a wink as together we held the band to the
music by the heartbeat of my mallet and his baton. But it
wasn't the same as our Easter concert. I mean, we had to
share the stage with a "Union Chorus, composed of local

church choirs" who sang Gounod's "Send Out Thy Light" and Christiansen's "Beautiful Savior." The songs lacked fun and to make matters worse, there were sermons by pastors and reverends that never seemed to end. One of the sermons was even called "The Cavalcade of an Idea," which didn't make any sense to me and probably didn't have a thing to do with the Bible.

The whole band was edgy and feeling strange but we didn't show it to the audience. When Mr. Jacques came back out from the wing and brought our instruments up everything came alive and fun again. The audience felt it too and showed it with their applause. I mean, how could the mumbo jumbo delivered by that flunky preacher compare with the great "Washington Post" march or just the mighty sound of a hundred thirty-three instruments splitting the air and thrilling the hearts of thousands of people under Mr. Jacques' snappy baton?

Oh, it was a busy fall schedule all right. Because just five nights later, on Friday, November 7, Protestants and preachers were replaced by clowns and variety acts, as we set the pace with music at the Fifth Annual Boys' Club Circus in Logan Heights. Wherever you turned you could see everybody was happy and free. There were clowns and jugglers and a unicyclist, and the famous Maurice Marmolejo of the Ringling Brothers circus who did a high wire act. Then a boy did a trick rope performance, and we saw a girl jump a horse through a fiery hoop. It was great being outside in the night air and when we played our special concert and made background music for all the variety acts we knew we were making everything better than it would have been without us. And when Mr. Bill Thompson the famous impersonator on the "Fibber McGee and Molly" radio program came out on our stage to do his act and gave us a big compliment, we knew we had earned it. After that we were back in the band hall or else on the Roosevelt Junior High School parade grounds sharpening our marching skills.

One day Mr. Jacques gave us all a talk. It was time, he said, to start selling tickets for our upcoming Tournament of Roses concert in Russ Auditorium. The proceeds would pay for our trip to Pasadena where we'd march and play in the Rose Parade. This was a good thing for us, he said, as we were ready now to sell ourselves and the band by personal contact with the public. What's more, it was a revered tradition of all the bands that had gone before us. When he handed out our packets of tickets to sell we saw the band's name printed on the tickets and were proud.

BONHAM BROTHERS BOYS BAND
PRESENTS
"*Tournament of Roses*"
CONCERT and STAGE SHOW
Friday Evening, December 5, 1947 — 8:30 o'clock
RUSS AUDITORIUM
Sponsored by the San Diego Junior Chamber of Commerce
Admission .83 - Fed. Tax .17 - Total $1.00

Nọ̄ 862

Selling our quota of tickets was a right of passage. Which meant that we'd take rank right up with the great bands that had gone before us. It also meant that we were becoming legitimate businessmen, paying our own way. And not only that, we were still showing all the makings of becoming the greatest of all the Bonham Brothers bands. So why not break the band's ticket-selling record by selling all our tickets in the shortest time ever? After all, there were other ways to show our greatness than by playing music, as even the band's motto and pledge said.

And so, for the rest of November, while we were learning the march medley "Illinois," and a new overture called "Omar Khayyam," and perfecting our marching, we set off each day after school in our uniforms and took the city by storm, combing neighborhoods, taking advantage of relatives, buttonholing everyone we could. Some boys went hog-wild and stormed whole business buildings downtown and made a killing. On November 21 the *San Diego Union* ran this article:

I have to admit I never got as worked up as some of the band members did. I mean, a doorbell was still a doorbell and a stranger was still a stranger, no matter how nice most of the people were. Besides, I was self-conscious about riding my bike around in my band uniform. And while I'm at it I might as well admit that the excitement of building my character, promoting civic spirit and boosting San Diego had worn off a little, which had probably been helped by a run-in I had with a man and his dog.

Boys Band Concert Tickets All Sold

All tickets have been sold for the Bonham Boys Band concert, sponsored by the San Diego Junior Chamber of Commerce and scheduled for Dec. 5, in the Russ Auditorium, George Hawley, chairman of the Junior Chamber concert committee announced yesterday.

"This is really a record," Hawley declared. "This is the first time in the history of the annual event that all tickets were sold as far as three weeks in advance of the performance."

The purpose of the program is to raise funds to send the band to Pasadena to participate in the Tournament of Roses Parade, where the group will march in front of the San Diego City and County float.

The Dec. 5 concert will be highlighted by the presentation of three acts of vaudeville and a performance by the San Diego State College majorettes, in addition to a varied musical program of the Boys Band, directed by Jules Jacques.

It happened one day after school when I had decided to wear my Levis and T-shirt and went out to see if I could still

sell the tickets that way. I only had a few left anyway and I figured in an hour I'd be all sold out. It was a beautiful Santa Ana
day and I sped north on Rosecrans Street along with the traffic, almost as far as the Loma theater, nearly two miles away.
From there I figured I'd start working my way back south
toward home just in time for dinner.

At the first house I parked my bike on the sidewalk and
strolled up a sloping walkway to the front door. Immediately a
little yippy-yappy terrier dog with an evil eye flew out from
around the corner of the house and took a bead on the back-
side of my legs. I turned around to face him and slowly backed
up to the front door and just when I turned my head to ring
the doorbell he sprang in for the kill. Wham! He got my right
calf where the bulge of the muscle is.

The dog's master came to the door, shooed off the little bas-
tard and told me he wasn't interested in buying any band tickets and to scram. My right leg bled all the way home and I
wished I'd had a baseball bat so I could kill the little mongrel.
I hadn't sold a single ticket either, and I vowed never to sell
another one unless it was to my Aunt Agnes and my Uncle Al
up in Los Angeles.

My mother blew her stack when she saw what had happened. She quickly dressed my wound, then piled me into the
car and drove to the man's house. I was glad too because the
old grump deserved one of my mother's tongue lashings. On
the way she warmed up by chewing me out for not wearing
my uniform, which she said was a sin against Mr. Jacques and
the band as well as a sign of shiftlessness and poor character.
Then we were at the scene of the crime and I was glad to be

off the hot seat. My mother marched up to the front door and rang the doorbell. The man opened the door. "Are you the owner of the dog that bit my son here?"

The man squinted at me. "I suppose so."

"You suppose so! What kind of an answer is that? I want to see that dog of yours. How do you know he doesn't have rabies? This boy here could be in trouble."

"The dog's okay."

"Okay, huh? Where's your proof of that?"

"He's okay."

"Listen here, bub, you'll get me proof of your nasty little dog's health or I'll put you in jail. If you think I'm kidding, you'd better think twice. And I want that proof and I want it no later than tomorrow evening. Do you hear me?"

The man shot a look at me then looked back to my mother. "You'll have it."

"Is that all you've got to say?"

"Uh, sorry."

"That's better."

The dog was okay and so was I, especially after seeing how my mother took care of the lousy bum who wouldn't buy a ticket from me or apologize for his crummy little dog. As for my remaining tickets, my father sold them to a couple of his friends at the cannery, which meant I didn't have to wear my uniform anymore or try to sell tickets to strangers. At least for another year, that is.

The concert was a great success. Everybody we'd sold tickets to came, even the people at the cannery who bought the tickets from my father, and we gave them all more than their money's worth. I mean, it was just like Jacques said. We were in business and what's more we all knew deep inside that we played better because of it. The "Star Spangled Banner," "Illinois," "Mt. Everest overture," "Omar Khayyam," "Washington Post"—who could top that? And then there was our Finale when three beautiful majorettes from San Diego State College strutted out on the stage and twirled their batons. Just looking at them made our hearts beat faster, which made me think back to when I had seen the trapeze girls at the Firemen's Annual Circus and Fireworks Show and how I'd wanted to run off with them and have them forever as my love slaves. The next day we were in the *San Diego Union* again.

2500 Attend Ninth Tournament Show

A crowd estimated at 2500 attended the ninth annual Tournament of Roses concert and stage show, featuring the 135-piece Bonham Brothers band, at Russ Auditorium last night.

George Hawley, Chairman of the Junior Chamber of Commerce Committee, in charge of arrangements, said that funds from the concert will be used to send the band to Pasadena to escort the San Diego float in the annual Tournament of Roses.

Jules Jacques conducted the band, which played a program of marches, overtures and novelty numbers. Featured were the xylophone trio, consisting of Jerry Hedrix, Buddy Recht and David Contreras, and Daniel Severns, sousaphone soloist. In the final number, baton-twirling State College majorettes, Marion Caster, Barbara Schmidt and Jo Ellen Weitzel, were featured.

Specialty acts included Valentine, Joan Derieux, in a staircase tap dance; the Four Staters Quartet, and Ralph and Lorraine, formerly of the "Song of Norway." Richard Nelson was master of ceremonies.

Never were we more in demand. The very next morning we rose early, put on our parade grays, and escorted Santa Claus from Lane Field up Broadway to Horton Plaza where he officially inaugurated the Christmas season in San Diego. Leading the band were Miss Marion Caster and her two companion majorettes, Miss Barbara Schmidt and Miss Jo Ellen Weitzel, the same majorettes who were featured with us the night before. There was a clown too, and a tiny Prince and Princess and the famous midget Chico Colla in his special tiny car. Thousands of San Diego children were waiting for us at the Plaza where there was a huge Christmas candle, two large Christmas trees and ten smaller ones, and plenty of other

Christmas decorations along with Santa's own personal throne. Mayor Harley E. Knox gave Santa Claus the keys to "every one of San Diego's chimneys." Then Santa went up and sat on his throne where he greeted all the children who stood in a long line and listened to their Christmas requests and handed to them gifts of candy and bubble gum and theater tickets. All the ceremonies were broadcast over radio stations KUSN and KYOR.

It was neat being part of all the Christmas spirit, even though we didn't believe in Santa any more, and it seemed that the words in the band motto about building better citizenship among boys was creeping into us pretty good. Six nights later, on December 12, we were escorting Santa again, this time in the annual Toyland Parade to inaugurate the holiday season for the North Park area. Thousands of children and their parents lined University Avenue from Boundary Street to Arizona Street to see Santa Claus and all the "story book floats," clowns, drill teams, bands, and drum and bugle corps. Along the parade route there were special Christmas lights and decorations and children squealing as forty fun-loving North Park Lions Club clowns handed out treats.

The next evening I was back out in the public again with the "little band" performing a Yuletide concert at the Army and Navy "Y." It was our last public appearance for the year and when we played "Anchors Away" and followed with the Army caisson song we could see the servicemen in the audience clapping. Some of them even stood up. There were a few though who just sat in their seats quiet and sad like. I could see them out in the audience and I knew it was because they weren't home with their families, or else they were thinking about their buddies who weren't coming home at all, or maybe about the Japs they had killed.

Then it was Christmas vacation and we began preparing for the Rose Parade. Mr. Harley L. Bonham came to see us in the band hall and told us all about the parade and said we had the band's great reputation to live up to. Then he said that we had proven our talent by playing in fourteen concerts, marched in nine parades, made music for a naval commissioning, and played patriotic marches for the Boy Scouts at the historic Camporee. As he spoke his head shook just like when he first spoke to us at his funeral parlor, but I knew now that it wasn't because of all the bodies he'd fixed up but because that's just the way he was. We were the very spirit of San Diego, he went on, and then he praised us some more. We had gladdened the hearts of San Diegans at two picnics and two circuses, he said, and entertained record crowds at the Del Mar Fair and taken a big part in a major charity football pageant. What's more we had crowned all the above by making history in a record-breaking reception for the returning war hero Admiral Chester W. Nimitz.

It was pretty amazing what we'd done all right, and it was easy to see how pleased Mr. Bonham was. Mr. Jacques too. He was standing behind Mr. Bonham next to the front entrance of the bandroom with his back to the wall. From time to time he'd look around the room at us but mostly he just kind of stared off over the heads of our clarinet section looking satisfied. Our next engagement, Mr. Bonham said, was a private affair, a tradition of the band, which we'd be celebrating at our upcoming second annual Christmas party concert at the First Methodist Church downtown. Of course we should not be unmindful, he said, of our first appearance for the granddaddy of all the parades that was approaching. The world-famous Tournament of Roses Parade in Pasadena, he said, was going to be an experience of a lifetime, something we'd never forget, something we'd always look back upon with pride. Then he told us that we had definitely earned this honor and that he was very proud of us.

I was twelve now, just one year away from being a teenager. It was sad in a way. I mean, when we played our Christmas concert on December 23 things didn't seem the same as they were a year ago. My heart didn't pound this time before the curtains opened, and I think it was the same with the rest of our band members. We were used to stage lights now and Mr. Jacques didn't have to give us that big smile or bring his baton down the way he did that first night when all our families and friends were out in the audience holding their breath and being just as nervous probably as we were. Something had drifted away, our kidhoods maybe, or just ignorance, or not knowing the score or something.

It was pretty much the same with the holidays too. I mean, I just couldn't get the Christmas spirit no matter how much I tried. Santa Claus didn't seem like Santa Claus anymore, and when I lay on the floor next to our family Christmas tree things didn't sparkle in me the way they did when I looked up into its tinsel and bulbs when I was a little kid. It made me sad thinking back on my mother and father holding hands by the tree on Christmas Eve at the Hayes house, and my baby sister and little brother, and our cat, Midnight, playing on the rug, and all my favorite bulbs and branches up in the tree. The bulbs were just bulbs now, bought by my mom in some department store, and I couldn't make friends with them anymore. Sometimes, especially when I was lying in bed at night thinking, I'd remember how grown-up people were said to lose their taste for watermelon and cantaloupes as they got older. Maybe it was the same with me, I thought. It was then that little waves of fear ran through me because here I was, trying to feel things, and they wouldn't come anymore.

Then Christmas was past and all of a sudden things seemed okay again. Mr. Jacques was drilling us hard, too. He had a twinkle in his eye and it made me feel good to hear him giving commands and things. For two straight days in a row we marched and played like crazy. Even the people at the zoo turned away from the camel exhibits to come and stand by the tall chain-link fence to watch us. On Sunday morning, December 28, the *San Diego Union* ran this article:

Bonham Boys' Band Practices

In preparation for this annual 6½-mile march in the famed Tournament of Roses parade New Year's Day, the 135-piece Bonham Brothers' band is undergoing a series of conditioning marches at the Roosevelt Junior High School parade grounds.

Jules Jacques, band director, said that the first march was held Friday and another yesterday. Others are scheduled tomorrow and Tuesday mornings from 9 to 10:45 a.m.

"The boys are getting in trim for the 3½-hour parade, Jacques said. "At the end of our practice marches, each of the boys will be ready to escort the Junior Chamber of Commerce-sponsored San Diego float."

Funds for the journey, to Pasadena and return by bus were raised at the recent Junior Chamber-sponsored Tournament of Roses concert in Russ Auditorium. The band will leave early New Year's morning and return the same day.

Our lines grew tighter. Our stamina grew. A new-found pitch and volume in our instruments was heard. Then it was New Year's Eve and we were ready to go.

It was all magic: leaving for Pasadena at 2:30 A.M. in four Greyhound buses with a police escort, and three hours later wolfing down a predawn breakfast in Whittier. A professional photographer took a picture of us all eating and I was the only one who looked up for the picture. Then we were on the bus again and it was starting to get light.

We unloaded the buses in Pasadena. It was exciting seeing all the floats and bands and horses getting ready for the parade along the residential streets, blocks away from the main parade route. The air was crisp and chilly and there were lots of beautiful majorettes twirling their batons and wearing Shako hats. Then from up front came the cry "Fall in!" and we were off, snare drums clicking, a hundred thirty-five boys in their white-and-blue uniforms, white shoulder straps and gold braids, all gig lines plumbed, caps squared off, smacking the street in unison in their polished white dress shoes.

No music yet, just the snare drums clicking the cadence. Up front four horses are click-clopping along under heavy carpets of silver. Behind us two more horses follow with their equestrian riders. Behind them the San Diego float is covered with jillions of gladioli, poinsettias, gardenias and roses. In their midst four pretty girls are finishing up practicing their poses of picking flowers. Then comes another float, smaller and covered with red carnations that spell out the theme of the float: "Golden West—Flower Basket of America." The red carnations are set in a background of chrysanthemums.

Another whistle blows up front and moments later we're making a left turn onto Orange Grand Avenue. Boom! The San Gabriel Mountains bulk tall and sharp ahead against the cloudless Southern California sky. Our drum section strikes up a snappy Collins six-eights cadence. Ahead the crowds are beginning to thicken along the sidewalks. Then comes the big moment and we're making the wide turn to our right and coming out onto Pasadena's famous Colorado Boulevard. The whistle sounds again. All instruments to the ready. Then we're striking up our first Sousa march and out of the corners of our eyes we can see the crowds clapping. We're definitely on Colorado Boulevard now and for a long way off we can see the parade route lined with people and the huge, caterpillar-like progression of bands, floats, drill teams, horses, cars, celebrities, ambulances, motorcycles, and cops.

After the Sousa march we snap back into another drum cadence. The band squares itself up. Then Jacques barks out a command and way up front Don Harrington raises his oversized baton and slams it down. Suddenly a hundred and thirty-five instruments are blasting out "California Here We Come." Another toot of a whistle and every boy snaps his head to the right. There on the side of the hill, the famous Elks Club going by, its members waving to us from the balcony, drinks in hand, looking gentlemanly in their suits and ties—still celebrating from the night before. They know who we are and we hold our eyes on them for another second. Then we're past. Snap! All eyes forward. Thundering applause hits us from both sides of the famous boulevard as we finish the song and bang into another drum cadence.

Seven glorious miles to go. Up ahead the slide trombones are leading the way. Then come the baritones and trumpets, followed by the drum section and tubas, then the saxes and piccolos with a sea of clarinets bringing up the rear. Another whistle blows. Up goes Harrington's baton again. Boom-boom! Boom-boom! Deep-roll boom-boom! And suddenly the air fills with Notre Dame's fight song. We're passing the reviewing stands and out of the corner of my eye I see the Channel 5 TV camera and a lot of flash bulbs popping.

Class! That's what we were. That and the imagination of Jules Jacques. At our first rest stop he brings us to parade rest, still as monuments, every eye staring straight ahead. Up front four aida trumpets flash to the lips of our best buglers. No martial stuff now. Instead it's "Mexicali Rose" sweetening the air. The crowds crane their necks to listen. Then a whistle sounds in the distance. The Standard Oil Company float ahead of us starts to move, then the horses, and we're off again, drums rolling, our lines straight as West Point cadets, and everyone behind us is buzzing with excitement and wishing we could have stayed.

Trumpeters to Herald Sunrise

From the stairway leading to the Organ Pavilion in Balboa Park, these trumpeters from Bonham Brothers' Boys Band will herald the sunrise at Easter rites tomorrow at 6:45 a.m. The boys, John Dawson, Merritt Canfield and Richard Bucey, left to right, also will appear on programs at 8 a.m. in Presidio Park and at the 10th annual concert of the band at 2:30 p.m. in Ford Bowl, also in Balboa Park.

Joo-o-les Jakes! His name rolls off my tongue and brings an affectionate grin. How he exploited us! And how we loved it! It was magic I tell you, showbiz, bigger than life. And it wasn't just at the Rose Parade either or when we were guests of the Rose Bowl and saw Michigan slaughter USC 49 to 0. No. It was everywhere we went that winter and spring of 1948. Were we playing a concert? Why not dazzle the audience with our tap dancing xylophonist, Buddy Recht, whose sights were already on Hollywood? Or maybe it was Bucey, our first trumpeter, and his sidekicks John Dawson and Robert Grimes accepting Jacques's invitation to rise, on the spot, and play the "Elena Poka" for everyone. Or our aida trumpeters standing on the stairway to the Organ Pavilion in Balboa Park, heralding the sunrise at Easter rites on Easter Sunday. Or when the newspaper reporters came to the band hall and Messrs. Naylor, Lauer and Lees were photographed tossing coins they'd collected from the band onto my overturned bass drum to buy milk for the hungry children in Europe.

THURSDAY MORNING, JANUARY 22, 1948

Boys Band Members Toss Money on Drum for Starving

Tossing coins on their bass drum, members of Bonham Brothers Band interrupt rehearsal to collect $5.15 to buy canned milk for European children. The trio, left to right, includes Ronald Naylor, James Lauer and Richard Lees. The band will march in the "Milk Ship" parade Saturday.

Oh it was magic, I tell you, the whole year, all of it. On January 24 we marched again down Broadway in another parade, this time before cheering crowds in the Milk Parade. Film stars Hedy Lamarr and Robert Cummings waved to us from the reviewing stands, and when we came to the Broadway pier we played a standing concert before a throng of San Diegans wishing well for the California goodwill milk ship *Golden Bear*, which was loaded with canned milk for the hungry European children.

A month later, on February 22, we were leading the way in the Mid-Winter Flower and Fruit Show Parade in Encinitas, the carnation capital of the world. Crowds cheered, pretty girls waved, and happy moms and dads held their children up to see. On March 21, on the vernal equinox, we again filled the Ford Bowl to overflowing for our second Easter concert. It seemed the whole city of San Diego came to hear us that day and we felt like pros and no one hit a single wrong note or missed a beat. The *San Diego Union* must have agreed because the next morning it began its coverage of us under the headline, "Bonham Brothers Boys' Band Gives Fine Easter Concert At Ford Bowl":

BONHAM BROTHERS' BOYS BAND GIVES FINE EASTER CONCERT AT FORD BOWL

BY CONSTANCE HERRESHOFF

A gala event of Easter afternoon was the concert played in Ford Bowl by the 136 young musicians of Bonham Brothers Boys Band, directed by the able conductor, Jules Jacques, now beginning his 19th season as director of this band.

A capacity audience turned out to hear the well-prepared program, made up of sacred musice appropriate to the Easter season, and lively marches and overtures, such as the "Coronation March" from Meyerbeer's "The Prophet," and Sousa's exhilarating "Stars and Stripes Forever."

A supplementary audience enjoyed this concert from the grassy slopes at the sides of the bowl and from the steps of the adjoining building. Some tardy motorists who had hoped to hear the concert left the scene because of the parking congestion.

The boys band deserves praise for its performance yesterday afternoon, especially considering that about half the players are new to the band this season. After playing 2 years with this band, the seniors drop out to make room for newcomers.

Popular ensemble groups heard in yesterday's concert were the Trumpet Trio composed of John Dawson, Richard Bucey and Robert Grimes; the Xylophone Trio, made up of Buddy Recht, Jerry Hendrix and David Contreras; and the Aida Trumpets, composed of Edwin Rappenhagen, Donald Cermak, Buddy Atwood and Henry Neal.

Daniel Severns' sousaphone solo was seen rather than heard, because the mike was picking up six piccolos and the ensemble instead of the sousaphone. Although the soloist seemed to be doing a good job, his "Solo Pomposo" came over in a soft and stealthy fashion, as though the sousaphone were taking part in a conspiracy.

Other soloists were Don A. Smith, tenor, with Diana Quint at the piano; and Alexander Ortega Jr., a 10-year-old pianist, who offered erratic interpretations of Lecuona's "Malaguena" and P a d e r e w ski's "Minuet." The tenor sang sacred numbers by unillustrious composers with conviction and ample vocal power.

After our Easter concert in the Ford Bowl we were booked solid for the rest of the spring: a special performance for the Hi Twelve at the Masonic Temple and Lodge in North Park (April 14); a concert at the Navy Hospital to conclude San Diego's celebration of National Music Week (May 9); a show and grand entry in the Hoover High School stadium for the first annual Boy Scout Circus (May 15); a park luncheon concert in Balboa Park's Pepper Grove for retired railroad employees (May 23); the annual South of Broadway Association Horse Parade (June 5); a concert for the Loma Linda College and Medical School in Riverside, California (June 13).

Then it was summer vacation and Mr. Jacques began conducting us in his short-sleeved sport shirts. It was fun practicing in the mornings instead of after school, and anyone could see that Mr. Jacques was having a good time, too. Sometimes he would put his baton down and pick up his trumpet to play along with the trumpet section, leaving the tempo of the band to me. It was a real honor to drive everyone on, not letting them drag or speed up, and I likened myself to a ship's captain and I wondered what Mr. Collins would think of me now.

Summer vacation. What joy! What freedom! No more class periods or suiting up for gym or having to lug home homework assignments I knew I'd never do, or report cards. Free to dive off the pier next to Jenning's Beach and do the crawl stroke out onto the bay where the PCs reached and tacked under the escarpments of the Point. Free too to play over-the-line at Cabrillo playground and afterwards fly home on my bike to eat tuna sandwiches and pick apricots off the tree in our back yard or shoot my BB gun at Coke bottles or if I was lucky to nail the big killer cat Jingle Bells when he made his rounds.

It didn't matter now if you had quit practicing on your rubber drum pad. The band was in me now, all the way down into my bones, and the chances of ever playing the snare drum again or mastering flam-a-doodles were pretty much over too. What I wanted now, and had earned the right to do, was to size up audiences when we played, especially the girls, and to be a person of the world. When we played two concerts on June 25—one of them in the morning at the Balboa Park Organ Pavilion for the California Purple Heart Convention, and the other in the afternoon at the San Diego Club for the San Diego Kiwanis—I couldn't stop grinning from all the power. The audiences shook their heads with admiration. It seemed they applauded longer, too, and everyone was talking about us afterwards.

It was the same four days later at the Del Mar Fair when we took to Stage B after the opening ceremonies and got the crowds going with a medley of marches. A sea breeze was blowing across the fairgrounds and we could hear cries and screams coming from the rides in the distance. Girls were everywhere too, and some of us who had higher seats kept a lookout for them. It was exciting to be looking sharp in our uniforms and being accomplished and knowing we could enchant all the people, especially the girls, and knowing that all this new power we were feeling was probably coming from the fact that some of us had pimples and were growing whiskers and when we talked our voices cracked when we least expected it.

After our opening medley a tall skinny man bounded up the stage steps and pulled the standing mike over to his mouth. Would the audience please welcome the lovely Virginia Mayo, queen goddess of Hollywood, the film directors' choice as the most beautiful woman alive? No sooner were his words out than I could feel her presence. Then I saw her dress out of the corner of my eye. She had come up into the band from the rear of the stage and was standing next to me, waiting to go forward to the mike, real close, only inches from my elbow! I could feel my face getting hot and my fingers tingling. A real living Hollywood movie actress! The hem of her beautiful white dress floated in the summer breeze, almost touching my leg. Go ahead. Don't be a coward. Look up into her face.

Maybe she'll see you and smile. Then she stepped forward through the saxophone section and I was destroyed.

No. 30,893   SAN DIEGO 12, CALIFORNIA, THURSDAY MORNING, JULY 1, 1948   *

County Agricultural Exposition Mecca for Horde of Pleasure Seekers

After a 6-day session with fat steers, small tots with too much ice cream and other Del Mar attractions, the cameraman took to the air to capture this overall picture of the San Diego County Fair. In these buildings and tents are housed exhibits and entertainment attractions which have been enjoyed by more than 190,000 persons. The exhibition will continue for 5 more days—through July 5.

After the Del Mar Fair we threw ourselves into summer vacation with a vengeance. I got myself a morning paper route, read the Hardy Boys, and in between practice sessions with the band swam in the bay, sailed sloops with my friend Phil Barber who had been tuna fishing and knew all about boats, and began building up my first fleet of derelict rowboats that I had rescued from the mud banks of Shelter Island. When I wasn't doing stuff around the bay I played over-the-line at Cabrillo, or else rode my bike up Cañon Street to the top of the Point and on through the woods of Madame Tingley's abandoned theosophical Institute to a sandstone bluff where I could watch the surfers riding the waves far below on their long balsa and redwood surfboards.

Three times a week I went to our morning practice sessions down in the bandroom. Jacques was teaching us new marches and fight songs. Days of happiness these were. Bliss by the car loads. Then one day late in July our parents received a brief note from Mr. Bonham:

July 23, 1943

Dear Parent,

Because of the polio situation and in order
to protect the health of the members of the
Bonham Brothers' Boys Band, there will be no
band rehearsal until further notice.

Sincerely yours,

Harley B. Bonham, Manager

It was the summer of the great polio scare and I'd never heard of iron lungs before or about the dread virus that could make my leg and nerve cells shrivel up. But what did I care? I was always outside and didn't go to pools or public places where I could come into contact with spit and goobers that kids left around.

Thus the summer passed, along with the polio scare, and I was never any freer or happier. But then just like all the other summers this summer too came to an end and I was back in school and a slave again getting colds from other kids, feeling my life dragging along, and fighting off going crazy from watching how long it took for the wall clocks in the classrooms to click off the minutes. Time turned into a giant soft, slimy snail just barely moving in contrast to the darting, beautiful, tiger swallowtail butterfly of speed it was all summer. On top of all this, they gave us homework which always made me say, "Why homework? They had us all day five days a week! What was the matter with them? They could have their stupid homework!" It was a patriotic duty in fact to not go along with it and anybody who cooperated and did homework I figured was a potential enemy and a traitor.

On September 11, 1948 we returned to the bandroom to prepare for the rest of the year. Jacques announced our fall schedule. It was loaded with challenges, he said. We would be pushed to new limits with tougher, more complex pieces. His face was tanner and more handsome than ever. Just being in the same room with him made me feel life flowing back into me.

The schedule was a challenge all right. Anybody could see that: the Moose State Convention Parade (September 24); the Second Annual Boys' Club Circus (October 1); the Shriner Parade and Football Classic (October 16); the Second Annual Reformation Observance in Balboa Park's Ford Bowl (October 24); the East San Diego Boom Daze Parade (November 6); the tenth annual Tournament of Roses concert and stage show in Russ Auditorium (November 13); the Second Annual Mother Goose Parade in El Cajon, (November 20); the Santa Claus concert at Lane Field followed by a parade on Broadway with movie notables Doris Day and Howard Duff (December 4); the Twelfth Annual Toyland Parade in North Park (December 10); the little band Christmas concert for the Armed Forces Y.M.C.A. (December 19).

With all that ahead of us we set to work mastering everything Jacques gave us, always remembering to strive after excellence and to distance ourselves from being ordinary, run-of-the-mill kids. Jacques seemed different, too. He was more serious, more elegant or whatever the word should be. It rubbed off on us, too, and when we went home to our dinners we felt richer and fuller inside, like we were blessed by something sacred that we shouldn't speak or brag about.

The people knew it too, even the newspaper writers. "Shrine Show Colorful. Rated Best in Contest's Eleven-Year History," the *San Diego Union* reported on October 17, and added: "The most colorful parade in the history of this eleven-year-old undertaking weaved its way up Broadway into the stadium. . . . During the halftime intermission, the Bonham Boys Band and the Hoover High drum and drill team shared field honors with the Aztec firedancers." On November 14 we were in the news again. Under the headline "Bonham Band Show Attracts Capacity Crowd" the *Union* reported: "A capacity crowd attended the Tenth Annual Tournament of Roses concert and stage show, featuring the 135-piece Bonham Brothers' Band, last night in Russ Auditorium." A lady who had heard us was singled out and quoted in the *Journal*:

Our self-esteem was at an all-time high. We heard people saying things like, "Just look at those boys. They march like professionals. They can play overtures and boleros and even boogie woogies in places like the Ford Bowl and the Russ Auditorium. And now

* * *

Mrs. Ethel (Aunty) Hafer, waitress in "218" Restaurant: "For several years I have seen the wonderful Bonham Brothers Boys Band in parades on Broadway, but Saturday night was my first time to hear them in a concert—at the Russ. One cannot say enough for the men who originated this now famous band. Such manly fellows are these band boys! I'd like to kiss every one of them."

* * *

look, they're off to the Rose Parade again. Yes sir, those boys are going places!"

Like the year before, we spent Christmas vacation marching ourselves into shape for the seven-mile-long, sixtieth annual Tournament of Roses Parade in Pasadena. The *San Diego Union* and *Daily Journal* came out to photograph us and do articles including one about Dean Stout losing his silver trumpet upon alighting from the outbound No. 11 streetcar at Park and University and how another youngster found it near where Dean had boarded the same streetcar and held it until he read a *Journal* notice of the loss and "set Dean tooting again." On New Year's Eve the *Daily Journal* reported:

Trumpetless

YOUNG MAN without a horn is 13-year-old Dean Stout, who lost his silver trumpet on San Diego's outbound No. 11 streetcar about noon Thursday and fears he won't get to march in the Rose Bowl parade at Pasadena Saturday unless it is returned to him. A member of Bonham Brothers Band, Dean missed his trumpet upon alighting from the streetcar at Park and University, and a search of the car almost immediately disclosed no trace of it.

Finds His Horn, Now He'll Blow

Young Dean Stout, 3692 Dwight, was up long before dawn today, a happy boy on his way to play his silver trumpet with Bonham Brothers Band in the Tournament of Roses parade at Pasadena.

Dean lost the trumpet Thursday. Another youngster found it near where Dean had boarded a street car and held it until he read a Journal notice of the loss. Then he set Dean tooting again.

Bonhams To Play In Rose Parade

Four special buses will take members of the 135-piece Bonham Brothers' Boys Band to Pasadena tomorrow for the San Diego organization's 11th appearance in the Tournament of Roses Parade.

The group will lead the Junior Chamber of Commerce-sponsored San Diego City-County float, depicting the world-famous local zoo, in the seven-mile long procession. After the parade, the boys will be guests at the Rose Bowl football game.

The parade was fantastic just like the year before. Everywhere you looked you could see the crowds. People sitting in the stands, people on the sidewalks, people leaning out of windows, people out on the edge of the boulevard being held back by policeman and officials. The Associated Press took a wire photo of us marching down Colorado Boulevard just after the big turn and you can see Mr. Jacques running ahead of us in his white parade suit and braided cap to push back the excited crowds that were disturbing our marching lines. Seven miles of glory it was. A record crowd of nearly two million. Afterwards we were honored as guests at the Rose Bowl game and saw the Northwestern Wildcats beat the California Bears football team 20 to 14. On the way home we stopped at Knott's Berry Farm in Buena Park to feast on its popular dinner of fried chicken, mashed potatoes and gravy, biscuits, and vegetables followed by hot boysenberry pie topped with vanilla ice cream.

The next day the papers said it all in a flurry of headlines:

San Diego Boys' Band Marches in Pasadena's Rose Parade

The Bonham Bros. Boys' Band of San Diego swings down Colorado Blvd. in Pasadena's annual Tournament of Roses parade.—(Associated Press Wirephoto.)

RECORD CROWD JAMS STREET FOR GAY PASADENA PARADE

Bright Floats Revive Childhood Memories

San Diego Takes Prize, Long Beach Sweepstake

Oh it was magic, I tell you, and the world was a wonderful place. We were growing up. And we had our great teacher watching over all of us to make sure we would.

Jacques continued to form us with touches that weren't to be found in our music books or even in the band's motto and pledge. Intangibles. Manly things. Leadership things. Things that inspired imitation. Like the day at practice when he stepped down off his conductor's platform and reached for Bucey's trumpet. Without a word he returned to the podium, quickly affixed his own mouthpiece, and commenced to belt out a few measures of Rimsky-Korsakov's "The Flight of the Bumblebee." When he handed the trumpet back, we all realized that no matter how good we were there was always room for improvement.

Another day he leaped off his dais, shoved a couple of our sax players aside, hurdled a bench, and knocked over a music stand to grab one of our baritone players. Poor wretch! He had leaned forward, thinking Jacques couldn't see him behind his music stand, and was smoking a cigarette. A cigarette no less. Bam! Up in the air he went in Jacques's powerful hands. The cigarette fell to the floor. "Pack your instrument and get out of here!" Jacques roared. "I won't let a bad apple spoil the barrel." Then stomping out the boy's cigarette on the old wooden floor of the band hall, he made his way back to the conductor's platform while the malefactor amongst us beat a retreat out of the bandroom with his head down.

Sometimes he invited guests to speak to us, former band members, composers, returning war heroes, symphony conductors, even a hypnotist once. All the while his guests talked he'd watch us, measuring our attentiveness and curiosity. Like the time he had the hypnotist come. Our minds were great tools, the hypnotist said, and could make things happen for good or for bad, depending on what we thought. The hypnotist was tall and skinny and looked like he could have come from a carnival show or a circus. But when he spoke we listened. Our minds, he said, were more powerful than matter. To prove it, he reached into his coat pocket and pulled out a giant hat pin and drove it straight through the soft part of his hand. His mind, he said, had told his hand that it wouldn't hurt or bleed. Everyone strained to see. Sure enough, there wasn't a drop of blood or anything. Then he showed us how he could hypnotize us if we wanted. We all watched as he raised his hands up and slowly started talking them down with deep calming words about how heavy and sleepy we were getting. I kept my eyes on his fingertips just like he said and after they were about half way down I started feeling really good all over. Then in the back of my mind I heard some of our drummers snickering and it was all I could do to fight off the sand bags of sleepiness that were piling up all over me. When I broke free I blushed and felt all puckery and out of the corner of my eye I could see that half of the clarinet section was already asleep.

That winter Jacques withdrew us from the public and took us to new heights by teaching us "The Great Century" march, "The Traveler" overture, another march called "Crosley," the overture "Narrator," and the beautiful overture "Diane," plus a sacred selection called "Eastertide." By the end of February we had them all mastered.

Sometimes Jacques celebrated our accomplishments with us. That's when he would reach for his trumpet, call for one of his favorite Sousa marches, and point to me to keep the beat. We'd play so loud it was almost wicked. Jacques's handsome face reddened as he faced his trumpet section and blew out the notes he'd played before any of us were born. When it was over, we'd all fall back from the power and glory of it and watch him. With a swipe of the back of his hand across his mouth he'd make a little flick of his trumpet and then place it down on his podium and give us his big handsome smile. It was the supreme compliment.

And it wasn't just things he did that put his touches on us either. It was things we heard or chanced to read about him. One day we learned that he had been bandmaster of the First U.S. Cavalry Band in World War I. Another day we were amazed to learn that he had played trumpet in the famous John Philip Sousa band. We also learned that he had been a member of the San Diego Symphony and before that had played in theater, even vaudeville orchestras. And way back before all that he'd studied under private teachers in Chicago, Illinois. It was all shadowy and wonderful and it made us stronger by adding to what we already knew and felt about him from our own experience.

All that winter we practiced in the bandroom. Some of us were even becoming geniuses. I remember when Jacques shut us all down and turned to the trumpet section. With a motion of his hand he invited Richard Bucey to stand and play the "Commodore Polka" for us. Another time he pointed to our saxophone septet and had them play "Zacatecas," after which they went on to play a medley of "Irish Songs." On another occasion I remember him turning to his right and motioning our trombone quartet to their feet to play "Stout Hearted

Men" and "Trombone Novelty." We all listened, and were proud, and no one ever got jealous.

Then it was spring again and somebody said we had finished our third year in the band. It was true all right. Plus we were teenagers now. And for some reason it was pretty much okay that we weren't kids anymore.

On April 17, 1949 we played our third Easter concert in the Ford Bowl. As expected the newspapers wrote us up big the next day. We had swelled Balboa Park's record post-war Sunday crowds by a turn-away throng of 5,000, they said. Nineteen band members were distinguished in solos, trios, quartets, quintets and septets that featured our trumpet, trombone, saxophone and drum sections. My old grammar school friend Donald Foster gave a flawless delivery of the band pledge. There were the usual sacred songs and an invocation, but everyone knew that we and not the Lord's resurrection were the real attractions of the popular event. When it was over the air was humming with our overtures and marches and you could see that the audience was leaving up the aisles full of inspiration and patriotic spirit.

After the Ford Bowl concert we were off and running in May, leading the National City Parade, then playing another concert for the Kiwanis in the San Diego Club, then entertaining thousands at the Family Fair in Balboa Park, the first of its kind in America. Then it was June and we were testing our endurance in the El Cajon Boulevard Parade (June 11), marching seven long miles to celebrate the completion of a synchronized traffic signal system along San Diego's new showpiece boulevard.

Our next date was a fund-raising concert for the upcoming September Knights Templar conclave in San Francisco. Everyone in the band was excited about it. We were business-men again and the money we were raising was going to pay our way to the big event and back. Knights would be coming to the great event from all over the country, too, thousands of them, as many as 35,000 some said, and that didn't include their families. Plus fifteen other bands would be performing during the great meeting. There would be a parade, too, and a huge pageant in the famous Kezar Stadium where the profes-sional Forty-Niner football team played. On top of all this we'd be given free transportation passes to ride the cable cars and see Fisherman's Wharf and the famous Golden Gate Bridge, the great Bay Bridge and Alcatraz. It didn't end there either. I mean, we'd be staying at the Embarcadero Y.M.C.A. right in the middle of the city with all its skyscrapers and be called "Sir Knight," which was an official title, probably because we were the personally chosen band of the national Knights Templar organization.

The fund-raising concert was given in Ford Bowl on the night of June 20 before a capacity audience of Knights, citi-zens, reporters, and city officials. Our band was down to 115 members now, lean and proud, and we were sharing the famous stage with stars from the Star-Light Opera Company. Just imagine that! One hundred fifteen kids good enough to play music for opera stars! That and the fact that we were rak-ing in the dough and paying our way to San Francisco. Come to think about it, maybe this was why we were at our greatest this night.

The program led off at 8:15 P.M. with our trumpeters Donald Cermak, Eddie Reppenhagen, Buddy Atwood and Henry Neal taking front stage to play the "Black Jack" march by Huffer. It was a different kind of beginning and we could feel the audience wondering about the big band sitting behind the trumpeters and when it would be coming in and what it would be playing. When our trumpeters finished their dazzling number the audience was really humming. Then Ronald Naylor, our Master of Ceremonies, strode proudly out to the mike to announce our playing of the beautiful overture "Diane" by Holmes. The evening, the audience, us, the music—everything seemed caught up in a spell or something. We all knew the overture by heart and when we played its last notes the audience broke into sustained applause. Then followed our saxophone septet of Bruce Beaman, Ralph Dilley, David Gill, Don Harrington, Ronald Naylor, Albert Smith and Donald Truesdale who played Sousa's "El Capitan." After that the audience fell into a moony spell as Miss Irene Cantos and Mr. Mike Bogle of the San Diego Star-Light Opera Company sang Friml's "Lak Jeem" and "Indian Love Call." Then it was us again. We played "Dear Old Nebraska U" and the audience swung along with us as though they were at a fall football game. Time flew. Everyone was having fun. The whole night was magic: Bucey quickly strutting out to the edge of the wide proscenium and playing "Stars in a Velvety Sky"; the novelty "Hank and Lank"; Miss Pat Thompson and Mr. Charles Cannon singing Herbert's "Italian Street Song" and Friml's "Symphony"; the band playing Fillmore's "Men of Ohio"; Buddy Recht tap-dancing his way out to the mike and wowing everyone with his tap-and-drum routine; Jacques trotting out to the podium to direct us in "Boogie Woogie Mice" by Paisner followed by "High School Cadets" by Sousa.

The spell of the June night held. A soft breeze off the bay played with our music sheets. A marine overcast kept the dew from falling. Then it was the Star-Light Opera Company's turn with Mr. Cannon singing "Riders in the Sky" and "The Donkey Serenade"; our xylophone quintette of Kenneth Bales, David Contreras, Jerry Hedrix, Buddy Recht, and James Recht playing "On the Square," "The Naughty Waltz" and "Invercargill." Finally Jacques came striding back to the podium and the next moment we were blasting along with our guest soloists in "Stout Hearted Men" and it was over.

Afterwards the magic of the night lingered long after the light of my bedroom was turned off. It was impossible to sleep. I lay in my bed listening to the sounds of the night and thinking of what we had accomplished that night. There was no doubt, we were the toast of San Diego. We had kept the tradition of the Bonham Brothers' Boys Bands. And of all our performances, this one on the night of June 20, 1949 was probably our greatest.

The next morning summer began and three days later we were the honored band at the Del Mar Fair Grounds, once again kicking off the County Fair with a concert to the huge crowds pouring through the main gate. It was our third and final appearance at the fair. We were the best band in the county.

July arrived and Jacques gave it to us as a vacation. I went bodysurfing at Pescadero beach, played baseball for the Post 6 Junior American Legion team, attended summer Bible school, read the books of Proverbs and Ecclesiastes, and paid no attention to clocks or calendars. Then, in the first week of August, we were back in the bandroom with Jacques really pouring it on. He was readying us for our homestretch, he said, as the great Band Number Seven. From now to our graduation next Easter we would have our greatest run, performing in twenty-two public engagements.

On the fourteenth of August we were back in the public eye, playing an outdoor concert in Balboa Park's Pepper Grove for the annual basket picnic of the Federation of State Societies. That same day we were bussed over to the other side of the park to play martial music at the dedication ceremonies for the new Boy Scout headquarters. On Friday, August 18, we were featured in Lemon Grove's first Community Festival Parade. The next morning we were marching down Broadway to lead the Parade of Bicycles. Oliver Hardy, the great comedian of Laurel and Hardy fame, marched on one side of us, and Bill Frawley the character actor marched on the other side. Behind us was a hoard of bicycled newspaper carriers from the *Union*, *Tribune-Sun* and *Daily Journal*, along with a host of Boy and Girl Scout units, Youth Hostelers, playground cyclists, the San Diego Cycle Club, and an open division in which anyone, young or old, could join.

Jacques drilled us like West Point cadets. There was always room to improve, he said, and he repeated this statement often. It was true too because after a while our lines held straight without our having to think about them. Thus on August 27 Jacques showed us off before 25,000 persons in the Thirteenth Annual National City Sports Jubilee Parade. A week later, on September 3, we were honored over all the other bands of San Diego at the city's historic "Fiestabahia" by marching to the summit of the new Ventura Bridge in Mission Bay Aquatic Park where we officially greeted a crowd of ribbon-cutting dignitaries at the bridge's public opening. Jacques raised his baton and brought it down, and we blasted out "California Here I Come." Then we played "The Star Spangled Banner" and our aida trumpeters followed with a fanfare, signaling the time for twelve aerial salutes to be fired, after which a parachute bearing the American flag floated down toward the bridge. Then came four F-86 jet fighters swooping over the bridge with a terrific roar just as Mayor Harley E. Knox cut the ribbon symbolizing the opening of the bridge and the start of the great event.

That afternoon I accepted a dare and swam all the way from Crown Point to Mission Beach, a distance of nearly two miles. I got pretty cold and when nobody could see me doing the crawl stroke I rolled and did the sidestroke. It took a long time to cross the bay and when I reached the far shore and staggered up the beach with a terrific stitch in my side I was greeted by half the band with cheers and hurrahs. Hey guys, how long before our next concert? Two hours, Billy. Great! And with all the cold and my stitch gone I struck off running, bolted across Mission Boulevard, turned right at the Belmont Park roller coaster, hurdled the sea wall, and sprinted down into the surf. The waves smashed and rippled against my ribs. Something inside me was screaming and laughing. I felt like Buck in Jack London's *Call of the Wild*. Our upcoming two concerts on Stage One at the west end of the Ventura bridge seemed far away, like they belonged to another time and another life.

On September 9, with only two days left before we had to go back to school, we marched in our parade grays in the huge Grape Day Festival parade in Escondido, California. All along Grand Avenue you could see the cheering crowds and gay decorations. There were lots of floats and horses and early-day stages and covered wagons and mule teams moving along with the jingle-jangle of their leaders' bells, along with a slew of farm wagons from the days when Escondido was just beginning. The seventeen-year-old fiesta queen, Gloria Billigmeier, rode on a float of grape vines and tossed dark Rose of Peru and muscat grapes into the crowds. That same afternoon we were picked to entertain the people in Grape Day Park where a giant barbecue was served and where numerous booths, educational and commercial, were set up.

And that was it. The summer of 1949 was gone, along with its fresh air and sea breezes and doing what I wanted to do and thinking about things and just being free. Now it was the other time, the time that hung still, the time that made me feel so cooped up and stifled I wondered sometimes how it was possible that I didn't go crazy. I never hated school more. It was like the Chinese water torture. Second by second, sixty seconds to a minute, sixty minutes to an hour—all in one spot—behind a desk in a row with a bunch of other slaves—all morning and into the middle of the afternoon—day after day, month after month. Sometimes the stupid thought would come over me that maybe there was something good about school that I had overlooked, something that I could fix my thoughts on, that I could take advantage of. But I never came up with anything. All there was was sack lunches and catching colds from other kids and sitting in Social Studies class and English class and suiting up for gym in little gray shorts and undershirts and having my attendance taken and being forced to strip naked and take showers with all the other boys and feeling embarrassed and degraded, and so on. The only relief came when the final bell rang and I could tear over the brush-covered hills for home and hop on my bike and haul butt off to Cabrillo playground to play flag football.

One fog-swept afternoon the terrible thing happened. We were playing two-hand tag football and I was making a dash around our right end when Noel Gomes broke through the line and landed on my right foot. Down I went with a dozen demons let loose in my ankle. Twenty-three chips and a couple of cracks, the doctor said. I'd be out of commission for eight weeks. Eight weeks! The San Francisco trip! I'd be missing out on the reward of all our practicing and marching, the trip of trips, probably the greatest out-of-town performance of the Bonham Brothers' Band in its history. The call to Mr. Jacques that night was grisly.

Funny thing though. I didn't miss the band. I hardly gave a thought about their performance at the Third Annual Boys Club Circus on the sixteenth of the month. Or two days later, when on a brilliant Sunday morning they boarded the train for San Francisco at the Santa Fe Depot. In fact, I was almost glad I didn't have to go. A voice kept saying inside me, "Your days of wearing uniforms and being in the band have served their purpose."

From our living room couch I watched the tunaboats and navy ships out in the bay and thought of Phil Barber's stories about tuna fishing. The pain of my broken foot drifted away. A new calling was ringing inside me. Visions of schooners and ketches, of tropical ports and the south seas had taken over. Kiwanis Clubs, parades, and concerts seemed a million miles away.

On September 25 the *San Diego Union* reported the story of the band's triumphant trip to San Francisco:

> * * *
> When the Bonham Band went to San Francisco as the Knights Templar band, they wore special capes with the insignia K.T. on them. Base drummer Billy Martin broke his ankle and didn't get to go. James Recht substituted for Billy. There were 15 bands from other cities there to attend the Triennial of Knights Templar. More than 35,000 members of this organization were present.
> * * *

The weeks dragged by. I hobbled over the hills to school and back on my foot-cast that came up to just under my knee. At home I read sports heroes stories and the Hardy Boys, memorized proverbs from the Bible, and toward the end of my healing time ventured back to Cabrillo playground and joined up with teams to play flag football while still wearing my cast. October came and went. Then on Friday, November 11, after having missed the band's participation in the pageantry of the Twelfth Annual Charity Football Game in Balboa Stadium, the Al Bahr Shrine Boom Daze Parade, and the Shrine Historical Days in Old Town parade, I was back with the band, testing my newly freed ankle as we boomed out our best marches in the Armistice Day Parade. Up Broadway we marched, from India Street to Fifteenth Street, and from there to Balboa Stadium, where we passed before a reviewing stand prior to disbanding. All along the way spectators lined the sidewalks five and six deep. Hundreds more could be seen filling office, store and residence windows. Sailors of the U.S. Naval Training center Battalion marched shoulder-to-shoulder behind their band which was followed by khaki-clad soldiers and mechanized equipment. Added to this six marines on top of an armored car recreated the famed picture of the American flag raising on Iwo Jima. Boy Scouts kept spectators back with staffs and ropes, then fell in at the rear to make up the last unit as the parade passed.

On November 19 we marched in the Third Annual Mother Goose Parade in El Cajon. A hundred thousand spectators watched as Santa Claus, clutching a bag of gifts, parachuted from a plane to land on an open field north of the El Cajon Theater. We led the key division, Division F, of the 12-division parade, with Santa riding directly behind us on his imperial throne on the Santa Claus float. There were sixty floats in all, each depicting a Mother Goose rhyme: the "Three Little Pigs," "Peter, Peter, Pumpkin Eater," "Hickery, Dickory Dock," "Little Miss Muffett," "The Old Woman in the Shoe," "Simple Simon," and so on. All along the parade route, from Lemon Avenue and Highway 80 at the western city limits to the intersection of Highway 80 and Main Street and past the reviewing stands before Lt. Governor Knight and other officials, we saw children being held up by their parents to see Santa. Jacques had a big Christmas smile on his face for the crowds and we all felt proud that we were chosen to escort Santa, and that our music excited the crowds.

Five days later, on November 26, on a foggy morning, we fell into ranks at Lane Field at a quarter past nine to open a free public program with a concert. Throngs of starry-eyed kids and parents stood and listened. Ed C. Learmont's animal act followed. Kids squealed over his elephant, four chimps and a trained horse. Then came the clowns and drum majorettes along with Cowboy Slim, aboard his horse. At ten o'clock sharp a giant blue navy helicopter came down out of the fog and landed on the field and out popped Santa Claus and the great happening was off and running.

After Mayor Knox handed over the key to the city to Santa, we serenaded Ol' Saint Nick who, they said, had an ear for music. Then we all formed a cavalcade and paraded up Broadway to Second Avenue, then on over to C Street and from C Street up to Seventh Avenue, then back over to Broadway and to the Plaza. The whole city it seemed had turned out. It was great having Santa right behind us on his special float and seeing all the nursery rhyme characters and balloons and children in gaily decorated small cars and huge candy canes marching alongside us. At Horton's Plaza, Hollywood stars Miss Margaret Whiting and Gordon MacRae combined their famous talents in greeting Santa Claus with Christmas carols, while behind them Santa's elves were hard at work making Christmas toys at the base of a 35-foot iceberg covering the fountain area and topped by a nine-foot candy cane.

It was our last parade on Broadway which was pretty sad when we thought about it. Pretty soon there'd be no more parades or concerts and we'd be on our own, having passed on the torch of "better citizenship among boys" to the youngsters coming up after us. In fact, on this very note Mr. Jacques had asked me to join him later that same day in taking part with the junior band in a huge competition up in the Ninth Annual All-Western Band Review in Long Beach. The junior band, he said, was a fine young bunch of boys, and had already shown great promise as a marching band. If they were to win the sweepstakes trophy, however, they'd need my strong command of tempo to hold them back from rushing the beat. He had already told them about me, he said. It would be a gift to them from Band Number Seven, a touch of class and authority these boys would never forget.

The honor was a very great one and when I thanked Mr. Jacques he said there was a good chance we'd win the Sweepstakes Trophy. The parade was drawing from all over the Western United States, he said, and San Diego alone had eighteen bands and drum and bugle corps entered. Just hold them back, Jacques said, nothing flashy, just the heartbeat, the old steady, authoritative heartbeat, and we could win. Years before a Bonham Boys' Band had won the All-Western Band Review Sweepstakes Trophy, he went on. Tonight, with my help, he'd like to repeat that honor. As it turned out, his wisdom and wish were granted.

At this time girls were starting to follow us around. Some of us even had fan clubs. One day before practice we saw some ninth and tenth graders gathered around Bucey up on Sixth Avenue at the top of the stairs to the bandroom. When we walked past him he stepped through the girls and gave us a big grin. "Howdy boys," he said. The girls giggled which made us tingle inside, like we were losing a part of our innocence or something. I mean, I myself was almost six feet tall now and I had strange new longings. I wanted to have a girlfriend bad. I wanted to break free and have new kinds of fun. The same thing must have been felt by the other band members because one day when we were warming up in the bandroom our clarinet section went crazy. Without warning they declared a pickleweed war against the trumpet and trombone sections. And just like that everyone piled out of the band hall to join in the fight.

Now it just so happened that at the bottom of the tiny canyon right outside the bandroom there was a patch of pickleweed about half the size of a tennis court. Right off spears of ice plant were flying through the air like missiles, scoring direct hits and leaving wound-points of green pickleweed juice on shirts and jackets. Then band members were yanking whole stems out of the ground and heaving them with terrific success, knocking other band members on their backs like upturned beetles in a growing swamp of crushed pickleweed juice. Then ranks closed and the throwing war degenerated into a wrestling match. It was then we heard the whistle. Every head turned. At the entrance to the band hall stood our master. He threw back his head, turned on his heel, and went inside with a big grin on his face. We all gathered ourselves up and trooped into the band hall like a gang of pirates after a barroom brawl. But our rehearsal that day was one of the best we ever had.

Winter weather was setting in when on the night of December 9 we marched for the last time in North Park's Annual Toyland Parade. Picture the scene: parents and children bundled up in coats, bonnets and caps against the threat of rain; floats galore; giant balloon figures—a 40-foot-long hippo encircled by a band of flowers, a dachshund as long as four automobiles, a piggy bank and a 65-foot Noah's Ark. There was a Humpty Dumpty and a Ferdinand the Bull; a fiery-tongued serpent with eighty feet of green tail writhing from side to side and threatening to scoop up a dozen or so children at a single bite; a sad-eyed donkey; a six-legged bug; a giant's head; king size lollipops, pumpkins, and candy canes and candied apples. Now add eight bands, clowns, drum and bugle corps units, and finally Santa Claus on his float, with us leading the procession behind a clown with a red lantern and a motorcycle police escort.

NO, HE WON'T BITE--HE'S JUST PARADING
One of the startling "participants" in North Park's spectacular Toyland Parade, marking the holiday season's opening, will be this Dachshund.

Eighty feet long, counting the loops, this rubber sea serpent will wind down University Ave. the evening of Dec. 9, one of 28 humorous monsters in the 10th annual North Park Toyland Parade. The serpent dwarfs its school-kid admirers. The parade will be 1½ miles long.

It was America in the last year of the forties, and we, the best boys band in the country, were featured in this, America's most quintessential parade. Right up North Park's University Avenue we went. Before us two band members carried our huge blue-and-gold banner with the words Bonham Brothers' Band on it. Standard bearer of twenty-nine proud years of tradition. Honest in all our dealings and thoughts. Clean of body and spirit. Forgivers, helpers and protectors of the weak, the young and old. Lovers of parents, home, neighbors and country. Always trying to be good students. Supporters of Sunday School. Polite and courteous at all times. Never failing to strive after harmony by good behavior and deportment. Yes, all that, and also pledgers of personal character building and better citizenship, along with being promoters of civic interest and boosters of San Diego.

At a rest stop we lowered our instruments. We could hear the crowds buzzing, the children squealing and laughing. Then a whistle blew and we came to the ready, and every ear heard it. It wasn't that loud actually, just a small pop and tinkle. Then the whistle blew again and we were off, keeping time to the latest Collins drum cadence. That's when I saw the shattered remains of the Seagram's bottle going by underfoot. You could smell the fresh whiskey too.

It was the unpardonable sin. Like spitting on your mom. Right in front of moms and dads and little kids, too. Even Santa Claus! Evil whisky befouling University Avenue, the Christmas Toyland Parade, God, country, apple pie. And from the Bonham Brothers' Boys Band yet! We marched on in shame. After the parade Jacques took the offending boy aside. A lot of us lingered to watch. We all went home worried.

At our next rehearsal we half-heartedly warmed up. An empty chair in the baritone section indicated who had done it. The time to begin rehearsal arrived. No Jacques. We sat silent. Then he strode through the front entrance and stepped up onto the podium. His face was serious. Our fellow band member, he said, was waiting outside. He had confessed his wrong and wanted to apologize to us. Jacques looked us over for a moment, then turned and went outside and brought the boy in.

His face was ashen. He stepped up onto the podium. He said he was sorry for what he had done. He loved being in the band, he said. Then his lips began to quiver. He put his head down and we could see his shoulders shaking. Then Jacques stepped forward and put his hand on the boy's shoulder. Most of us had tears in our eyes, a few cried out, some even cheered.

On December 17 we made our final appearance at Russ Auditorium. We were no longer boys now and on some of us our uniforms didn't fit very well, but no one saw or cared. From the opening number we held the audience in our power: Jacques in his resplendent white conductor's suit leading us off with "Marcho Poco" and "Olympia"; then Bucey and Weid stepping into the spotlight and playing de Ville's stirring arrangement of "The Swiss Boy"; then the band playing Sousa's "Rifle Regiment," after which our five xylophonists wheeled out their instruments to recreate with their soft mallets the haunting strains of "Independentia," "Popular Medley" and "Bolero."

The junior band in the orchestra pit below us sat in awe as they waited their turn to be introduced to the San Diego public. More than once applause erupted during the program's special features: Ted Otis, the world famous baton twirler, dazzling everyone with his performances with first one then two and finally three batons at once; the boy wonder Alexander Ortega playing Kochaturian's "Toccata" and Rachmaninoff's "Prelude" in C# Minor on the piano; the adagio dancers Shannon and Gaye; the musical personality Larry Collins. But the applause was loudest and longest when Jacques returned to the podium to conduct us in "El Dorado" and "Jalousie." Buddy Recht followed with his new routine "Grandfather's Drum," after which our trombone quartet of Fred Bliss, Roderick Savary, Gale Seevers, and William Barend marched out under the lights, trombones glistening, to play Fillmore's "Lassus Trombone."

For our finale, "The Spirit of Christmas," Jacques asked the junior band to rise from their seats to sing a selection of Christmas carols led by J. O. Hedwall of the University Christian Church. It was the perfect touch—innocence, nostalgia, hope, sweetness all wrapped into one. Then it was over and the stage curtains were sweeping across the stage.

None of us wanted to leave afterwards. The young members of Band Number Eight came up to meet us. We congratulated their caroling and sweepstakes prize, gave them advice, and told them stories. On December 22, just five more days from now, we'd be sharing the stage with them in our annual Christmas Party concert at the First Methodist Church downtown, playing the first half of the program with our favorite marches, overtures and Yuletide selections.

Then it was New Year's Day 1950, the beginning of a new decade, and we were proudly off, marching for the last time down Colorado Boulevard in the Rose Parade. Under an overcast sky we struck up "California Here I Come" and moments later snapped off a final salute to the Elk's Club. Behind us rolled the San Diego float that had won the President's Trophy, covered with 7,000 roses and bearing the logo "Birthplace of California." Along the famous boulevard a "record smashing" two million people cheered as we played solos on breaks, tapped out Mr. Collins's drum cadences between marches, and split the air with the strains of Sousa, Bennett and Fillmore.

It was our last hurrah. Before the parade Don Harrington jumped up on a bench in the basement of the Pasadena Elk's

Club and gave a muscle-posing exhibition while we were changing into our concert whites. Not to be outdone I set a band record by carrying the bass drum the whole seven mile parade route without switching to the cymbals for relief. And Jacques, resplendent as ever in his white conductor's suit, strutted along next to our right corner trombonist, snapping his arms across his body in the tradition of the World War I bandmaster. After the parade we were complimentary guests of the Rose Bowl Game for the third straight year where we saw Ohio State beat California 17 to 14.

Largest New Year's turnout in the history of American football, 100,963 spectators, jammed the Rose Bowl yesterday to see Ohio State's 17-14 victory over California.—Associated Press Wirephoto.

After the game we piled into our buses like conquering heroes and Jacques treated us to our traditional fried chicken dinner at Knott's Berry Farm in Buena Park on our way home.

Joo-o-les Jacques! How he loved us, and how we loved him back. That winter he withdrew us from the public one last time, taking us to our greatest heights as we mastered "The Forty Thieves March to the Cave, and Depart" and "The Coronation" in V. F. Safranek's suite: An Arabian Night. To these sophisticated selections he added J. J. Richard's "New Freedom March," "Charlemagne," and "Bonham Brothers' Band." For flare and brilliance he had us learn Walters's difficult syncopated novelty "Bandinage for Brasses." All our rehearsals now were in the bandroom. It was just us and him. Sometimes he would put his baton down, like old times, and play his trumpet with us, leaving the heartbeat of the band to me.

By spring he had finished his work. We were now 104 members strong, the crème of the crème, ready to graduate into the world of men and manners. Four years had passed since we had seen Mr. Jacques holding his watch chain and asking us how strong it was. All the rest of our lives we would cherish our memories with him; his disciplinings, his waving of his trumpet to make a point, the way he watched us when we had guests, the tapping of his baton that meant we had to begin again, his passionate words when we did poorly or well.

At unexpected times the reel of memories turns, flashing those enchanting images that forever keep old hearts young. Then it is that we see the glint of brass under the stage lights, the waving crowds, all sunny and smiling, the Elks standing on their balcony in their business suits; the play of shadows under the pepper trees in Balboa Park, and Santa riding in the Toyland Parade, remembrance of the Queen of the Grape Day Parade tossing grapes into the crowds; the exciting blue-and-white of our uniforms lifting and falling to John Philip Sousa's marches as we passed in review before celebrities and TV cameras; the hum of summer crowds, the smell of sea breezes at the Del Mar Fair; the first coming together of our instruments down in the holy of holies we called the bandroom; the night we put on our new uniforms and looked back at ourselves in the mirror; the terror of our first concert; and, magically crossing the stage that long ago night, our great leader banishing with a smile and a flick of his baton all our fears and handing to us the world.

Easter Sunday 1950. Before us a sea of white, a glorious spring day, the Ford Bowl jammed to overflowing. It was our final Easter concert, our graduation, the end of an era. Jacques smiled a different smile now, and we could see a trace of sadness in his eyes. It was the last time we would be together. We played from memory. It was just us and him.

The audience was swept away. Everything that a band should be filled their ears, inspired them to passionate applause, even cheers. The ghosts of Sousa and Bizet and other immortals moved among us. The sun beamed down, the earth spun, the sky smiled . . .

I shall never forget what Jacques said to me afterwards. He had come into our midst and was saying his farewells. I stood watching. There was a lump in my throat. Then he stepped between two saxophone players and approached me. For a moment our eyes locked, just like the night when we first met.

"William, you have been one of the most loyal band members I've ever had," he said. "I'm very proud to have worked with you."

"Thank you, Mr. Jacques . . ." My throat was too tight to say anything more. He reached toward me and put his hand around my arm. I could see the brown specks in his eyes.

"Good-bye, Bill, and good luck to you." He turned and went over to some other band members. I looked out into the audience and found my family. They were standing and talking in the bright afternoon sunlight. My mother had been watching. She waved and I waved back.

30361485R10051

Made in the USA
San Bernardino, CA
24 March 2019